The
Relentless
Reds

hal mccoy....text

earl lawson....foreword

pete alexis....player profiles

dennis gruelle....photographs

susan p. arena....production supervisor

Published by PressCo, Inc., Shelbyville, Ky.
William E. Matthews, President and Publisher

table of contents

dedication

to the 1975 world champion cincinnati reds...

and to their legions of followers who waited so long

introduction

by bill matthews

Trying to get from Shelbyville, Ky., to Cincinnati, Ohio, in 1940 was not an easy assignment, especially for a 10-year-old boy starstruck on something called baseball and, in particular, on a team called the Cincinnati Reds.

It was considerably easier to listen to Roger Baker and Dick Bray describe the day-to-day thrills as the Reds, led by Bucky Walters and Paul Derringer, and by Ernie Lombardi, Ival Goodman, and Frank McCormick, edged the Brooklyn Dodgers of Whitlow Wyatt and Hugh Casey, Pee Wee Reese and Dolph Camilli, for the National League flag.

The World Series? Even a 10-year-old had to know that he was listening to one of the most memorable ever as that same Walters-Derringer duo each won two games to finally whip the heroic Bobo Newsome and the Detroit Tigers four games to three.

Looking back, now, that fall of 1940 was even more significant not only to a youngster in Shelbyville, but to millions of Cincinnati Reds fans everywhere, because, without it, all they would have had to remember in the way of World Series titles was the infamous get-together of 1919 when the ''black sox'' went ''on the take'' and made hollow the Reds' cry of world champions.

That 1940 championship preceded by slightly more than a year a stark morning at Pearl Harbor which not only ultimately changed the world's shape, but also that of baseball. Many professional players summoned to fight never returned, and many of those who did had sacrificed their peak years, and thousands of hits and homers to Uncle Sam. Mize, Slaughter, Williams, the Dimaggio brothers, Case, Musail and many others would never establish all the records for which their brillance had seemingly destined them. But at least they came back.

The Reds were a mediocre wartime team, and most of the club's pre-war stars had retired or were over the hill when the hostilities ended.

Night baseball, still something of a rarity before the war, became an important force in entertaining factory workers grown weary of making war machines.

After the war came two enormous changes -- television and the black breakthrough. Television took the game into millions of homes whose occupants had never seen more than a Kitty League game in Fulton, Kentucky, a Pacific Coast League game in Seattle, or perhaps a Sally League encounter in Savannah.

Jackie Robinson, followed by Larry Doby, Luke Easter, Monte Irvin, and many others, added an exciting new dimension to the game, and gave baseball a long-missing social consciousness.

But in an era marked by change, the Reds played with remarkably consistent mediocrity. From 1946 to 1955 the team finished no higher than fifth, and fans laboring through the 10-year period of monotony had few thrills. At least there were some, including Ewell Blackwell's near consecutive no-hitters in 1947, Ted Kluszewski's booming home runs into the sundeck, and Kenny Raffensberger's dipsy-doodlers. Years of watching a seemingly unending "wave" of .240 hitters was underscored most vividly in a teenager's mind on one particular Sunday, July 4, 1949, when the Reds lost a twinbill to the Pirates 2-1, 1-0, with Walker Cooper's homer accounting for Cincinnati's lone score.

1956 brought an awakening, heralded by a sure-stroking outfielder named Frank Robinson who teamed with Kluszewski and Wally Post for 109 home runs [Gus Bell added 29 and Ed Bailey 28] to drive the team to within two games of Brooklyn at the finish. From a good pitch -no hit club, the team had suddenly become one of good hitting and little pitching.

From 1956 through 1965 the Reds were consistent contenders, with a National League flag in 1961 the benchmark in the illustrious managerial career of the late Fred Hutchinson.

But disillusionment set in following the trade of Robinson at the end of the 1965 season and the team fell to seventh the following year.

When managerial front office whiz Bob Howsam was lured away from St. Louis to take charge of the Reds in early 1967, the city's interest in the game had reached its lowest ebb since the lacklustre 40's.

Howsam did not find a club without talent. Pete Rose had arrived in 1963, Tony Perez in 1965, and Johnny Bench was to become a fixture in 1968. But changes obviously had to be made, and Howsam made them, trading away or shuffling to the minors the malcontents and "losers". He wanted a winner, and stressed from the start that winners not only played that way on the field, but looked and acted that way off the diamond.

In nine years Howsam, with Sparky Anderson assuming charge on the field in 1970, changed Cincinnati's image from that of late season collapser to that of Playoff Champs, National League titlists, and, finally, World Champions.

The 1975 World Championship resulted not only from the hard work of Bob Howsam, his front office, and 25 Reds, but from the vision of a group of Cincinnatians, headed by Francis Dale and Louis Nippert, who bought the franchise and kept it in Cincinnati when the game's future in the Queen City had become uncertain following the debacle of 1966. These men had faith not only in baseball, but in the future of one of America's greatest cities.

1940-1975 -- Thirty five years of ups and downs for baseball in Cincinnati, mirroring all too accurately the upheavals of the game itself and the world at large. And yet with all its external changes, the game itself and the skills required have undergone remarkably little alteration, testifying to the intrinsically perfect form of competitive challenge which it presents -- to pitcher, batter, and fielder. Its basic strength and integrity have even served as a unifying force, as in Detroit in 1968 and Pittsburgh in 1971, for citizens otherwise divided on the great social issues of the day.

For consistency of excitement and brilliance of performance, the 1975 World Series stands out as perhaps the greatest ever played, certainly rivaling, if not surpassing, the Pirates-Yankees clash of 1961 and other notable fall classics.

More than anything else this book focuses on those seven dramatic games in October 1975 which left more television watchers bleary-eyed, awe-stricken, and sleepless than any sports spectacle in history.

That 10-year-old kid of 1940 is 45 now. His frustration, his suffering -- and that of millions of Reds fans -- through 35 years has ended. However bittersweet the memories of those 35 years might have been, all were washed away in Boston on October 22, 1975, in a sea of un-relenting emotion which only those who have suffered the longest can appreciate with fullest intensity.

foreword

by earl lawson

As the train rumbled along the tracks carrying the Cincinnati Reds from Pittsburgh to New York, Rocky Bridges gazed out the window of the club car.

"Oh, oh," exclaimed Rocky, spotting the ruins of what once was a brick schoolhouse, "some kid must have flunked chemistry."

The time was the early 1950's. Unlike today's 1975 World Champion Reds, the Cincinnati players of some 25 years ago drew more laughs than fans. They didn't have great talent, but they did have a great sense of humor.

Bridges, for instances, will never make it to the Hall of Fame. But some of his classic one liners will live as long as the game of baseball.

"Geez, Rocky, if you're gonna chew tobacco at least learn how to spit over your chin," teammate Grady Hatton once remarked disgustedly as he focused his eyes on the stained front of Bridges' uniform shirt.

"I can," was Bridges' unhesitating response. "It's just that sometimes the wind is blowing the wrong way."

There weren't any aces on the Reds' pitching staff in the early 50's, but there were a lot of jokers. Art Fowler, a country boy from Converse, S. C., was one. Frank Smith, a side-arming right handed relief pitcher, was another.

Fowler, who was 30 when he first made it to the major leagues, liked his beer almost as much as a victory. One night as the Reds stopped off in Lynchburg, Va., for an exhibition game with the Washington Senators, their traveling companions en route home from spring training, Fowler dropped into a local tavern to down a few.

One beer, as well as one word, led to another. And, it wasn't long before Fowler was involved in a little hassle with a few of the local citizenry. Fortunately, a few of Art's teammates wandered into the tavern, quickly surveyed the scene and whisked Art back to the train.

"You know those guys you were squabbling with weren't exactly midgets," Art was reminded. "You could have wound up getting worked over pretty good."

"Shucks, size don't make no difference," replied the unabashed Fowler. "Why I once saw a little ole honeybee chase a 1000 pound bull all around a pasture."

No one hated the running exercises required of pitchers more than Fowler.

"If running were so important," he'd tell you in a southern accent as thick as molasses, "then Jesse Owens would have been a 20-game winner."

So, it was surprising that Fowler later wound up as a pitching coach under Billy Martin when the latter managed at Minnesota, Detroit and Texas.

One of Smith's favorite pastimes was relating ficticious episodes he experienced during a World War II in which he never participated. And, one of Frank's most avid listeners was Hobie Landrith, who, at the time, was a young Red catcher not too many years off the Michigan State campus.

Landrith would listen wide-eyed as Smitty told of an escape from a German prison camp. For hours the fun-loving Red relief pitcher would drag out his story. As the suspense mounted so did Hobie's interest.

Now Smith was racing across an open field amidst a hail of machine gun bullets. Freedom was only a few hundred yards away.

"What happened, what happened?" exclaimed Landrith.

"What do you think happened? I got killed," answered the unsmiling Smitty.

Landrith had received his baptism as a major leaguer.

Surprisingly, Fowler couldn't drive an automobile when he first joined the Reds.

"But I can guide one," he'd proudly tell you.

After a couple of years with the Reds, Fowler learned to drive. What's more, he purchased a somewhat battered 1952 used car and headed for his Converse, S. C. home after the 1955 season.

"You'll never make it home in that heap," taunted Fowler's teammates.

As usual, Art wasn't without a comeback.

"What do you mean?" he asked. "Why when I get home and the folks take a look at this car they'll think I'm Dizzy Dean. Why down home they ain't even seen the 1951 models yet."

If Smith had been as quick with his fast ball as he was with a quip, he'd rated alongside Bob Feller.

No one who was there will forget the day during the 1954

season when the Dodgers' Carl Furillo tagged Smitty for a grand slammer, a smash which bounced off a billboard that adorned the rooftop of the laundry which once stood beyond the left field fence at old Crosley Field.

Rogers Hornsby was the Reds' manager that season.

Having retired the side after Furillo's grand slammer a none-too-happy Smith had trudged toward the Reds' dugout.

"Smitty," asked Hornsby as Frank reached the dugout steps, "was that pitch to Furillo a good one?"

"It sure as hell must have been, he hit it far enough," answered Smitty.

In the spring of 1956 one year after Birdie Tebbetts had succeeded Hornsby as manager of the Reds a 20-year-old youngster who two years ago became the first black manager in the history of the major leagues made his first appearance at the Reds' Tampa, Fla., training camp.

Frank Robinson's legs were so skinny they'd earned him the nickname of "Pencils" during his years at Oakland's McClymonds High School. But, from the waist up, Robby's muscular body looked as if it had been hewed by the tools of a sculptor.

That first season Robinson slammed 38 homers, tying a record for rookies which had been set by Wally Berger. And, in doing so, Robby led a fence busting crew of Red sluggers who socked a record tying 221 homers while finishing third, just two games out of first place.

Big Ted Kluszewski, whose bulging biceps created almost as many oohs and aahs among Red fans as the shots off of his booming bat, was the elder statesman of that 1956 Murderous Row which also included Wally Post, Gus Bell and Ed Bailey.

Unfortunately, the Reds that year didn't have the pitching to match their hitting. Brooks Lawrence, acquired from the St. Louis Cardinals for a pint-sized lefty named Jackie Collum, who quickly faded into oblivion, was the top winner with 19 victories. Hershell Freeman, acquired from the Boston Red Sox for the $25,000 waiver price, was second to Lawrence with 14 victories.

Five years later Robinson, arrested on a concealed weapons charge some three months before the season's opener, silenced his hecklers by leading the Reds to their first pennant in 20 years, collecting the league's Most Valuable Player Award along the way.

William O. DeWitt, who later was to become owner of the Reds, had taken over the club the winter of 1960, replacing Gabe Paul, who had been given an offer by the Houston club that a guy just couldn't refuse.

And, it was a three-way trade negotiated by DeWitt and involving the Reds, Braves and Chicago White Sox which played as big a role in the club's winning the 1961 pennant as Robinson's heroics.

In exchange for pitchers Joey Jay and Juan Pizarro, the Reds sent shortstop Roy McMillan to the Braves. DeWitt then packaged Pizarro with veteran right hander Cal McLish and sent the two to the White Sox for third baseman Gene Freese.

That spring of 1961 the Reds had looked like anything but potential pennant winners as they floundered their way through their Grapefruit League schedule.

"I can't believe these are the same players who told me they were so good at contract time," an exasperated DeWitt had exclaimed as he watched a particularly dismal performance by the Reds during an exhibition game with the St. Louis Cardinals one sunny afternoon in St. Petersburg, Fla.

But come the end of September the "Ragamuffin Reds" as they had become to be known around the league somehow had managed to outlast the Los Angeles Dodgers to win the pennant and precipitate a downtown pennant celebration which dwarfed New Year's Eve demonstrations of past years.

But, even before all of the hullabaloo had subsided the New York Yankees had annexed the World Championship by taking four of five games from the Reds.

Three years later the Reds were back in the thick of another pennant race. After winning nine in a row they found themselves leading the National League by one game with five games remaining in the regular season.

But, as fate would have it, the Reds wound up losing four of those five games and finished tied for second place with the Philadelphia Phils, one game behind the pennant winning St. Louis Cardinals.

In the winter of 1966 DeWitt, who had purchased the Reds from the Crosley Foundation, sold out to a syndicate, comprised mainly of Cincinnatians and headed by Francis L. Dale, then publisher of the Cincinnati Enquirer.

The new Reds' ownership, using a lucrative contract as bait, lured Robert L. Howsam from the St. Louis Cardinals to serve as the club's new general manager.

Howsam, with holdovers Tony Perez, Pete Rose, Tommy Helms, Lee May, and Johnny Bench as a nucleus, began building a team which was to earn the nickname, "The Big Red Machine," as it rolled to the National League pennant in 1970 by making a runaway race of the western division and then sweeping the playoffs from the Pittsburgh Pirates in three games.

But, just as they did nine years earlier, the Reds proved to be easy pickings in the World Series, again losing in five games, this time to the Baltimore Orioles.

Two years later the Reds again were back in the World Series. But again the World Championship eluded them as they lost to the Oakland A's in seven games.

But the Reds weren't to be denied.

In 1975 the Reds won their fourth divisional title since moving into Riverfront Stadium.

Again they won the playoffs, sweeping the Pittsburgh Pirates in three games. And, in perhaps the most exciting World Series in baseball history, the Reds then went on to beat the Boston Red Sox in a seven game series to give Cincinnati its first World championship in 35 years.

In the pages which follow, Hal McCoy, the Dayton Daily News award winning sports writer, enables the reader to relive with the players that glorious season of 1975.

You'll slide into second base with Joe Morgan and roam the outfield with Cesar Geronimo. You'll experience the shoulder pains of Johnny Bench. And, you'll share the elation of Gary Nolan, making a comeback after two years of inactivity. You'll feel the sharp needle point of Tony Perez, the team's No. 1 clubhouse agitator.

You'll find yourself rooting for Pete Rose to get that 200th hit he cherishes so much. And, you'll share the thrills of rookies Will McEnaney and Rawly Eastwick as they participate in their first pennant race.

And, when you put down the book, you'll be convinced that if the relentless Reds aren't the best team in the club's history, then surely they're the gutsiest.

COLD WEATHER DECISION--It was on a chilly Friday in May that Sparky Anderson finally decided to shift Pete Rose to third base.

chapter one

It was a misty midwestern May day on the north bank of the Ohio river. A man standing outside Cincinnati's Riverfront Stadium found it difficult to peer through the fog and catch a glimpse of the Mike Fink riverboat restaurant, anchored on the south bank in Kentucky.

The dreary day was enough to lower the spirits of the most cheery of men, but the cold, black numbers in his newspaper made it even a more listless day for George "Sparky" Anderson. The baseball standings weren't pleasant for the manager of The Big Red Machine, a self-addressed nickname the players have given the Cincinnati Reds.

"Cincinnati: 12-12 .500," the newspaper told Anderson. Sparky tossed aside his newspaper and dropped his chin in his hand, drumming nervous fingers on his clubhouse office desk. What to do, what to do? The Los Angeles Dodgers were already constructing a lead on the Reds and the fans, knowing their Cincinnati team had the best athletes in the National League, were already getting restless. Every time Anderson popped his white-thatched head out of the dugout, his ears burned with cascading boos.

It was May 2, a chilly Friday, and the Reds were taking batting practice before a night game with the Atlanta Braves. Captain Pete Rose, Cincinnati's left fielder, was fooling around with a first baseman's mitt, taking grounders and receiving throws at the bag. "The perfect opportunity," Anderson thought as he spied Rose.

The Reds were getting absolutely no offense out of third base, a position being handled at the time by a committee. Any able body would do, but there didn't seem to be an able body. And, sitting on the bench was outfielder George Foster, a man with gargantuan strength and an untapped body full of potential.

"You can't play there at first," Sparky yelled at Rose.

"I sure can," said Rose, digging a throw out of the dirt.

"Can you play there?" Anderson asked, pointing across the AstroTurf to third base.

"Anywhere you want me to play," Pete said.

"Throw away that mitt and get yourself an infielder's glove," Anderson yelled matter-of-factly. Turning to mammoth Ted Kluszewski, Cincinnati's batting instructor, Sparky said, "Pete's gonna try third. Why don't you hit some grounders to him."

The next night, Peter Edward Rose was a third baseman. A few games later, George Foster was in left field. And, on May 18, the Reds sent infielder John Vukovich to their Indianapolis farm and called up Rawlins Jackson Eastwick III, a 24-year-old relief pitcher who turned into Cincinnati's late-inning stopper.

Rose spent hour after hour taking ground balls at third and making throws to first, many hours before the rest of the team arrived at the ball park for games. He made so many throws he strained his arm and the soreness remained all season, but Pete remained at third base.

While Rose made the adjustment, the Reds floundered along at .500, reaching 20-20 on May 20, five games behind the Dodgers. Then, it happened.

Relentlessly, they won. And won and won and won.

"It got so we came to the ball park not expecting to win, but knowing we would win," said catcher Johnny Bench. "It was an eerie feeling. You could sense something big was happening." The Reds put together a streak that has seldom been matched in baseball. They won 41 of their next 50 games up to the All-Star break, making up 17½ games on the Dodgers to take a 12½-game lead.

During those 50 games, Rose zinged 70 hits and his batting average climbed from .308 to .319 as he hit safely in 41 of those 50 games. And, he didn't make an error at third base. Nobody was making many. The Reds set a major league record by playing 15 straight errorless games, 152 innings, 635 chances. "When people think of the Big Red Machine, they don't think about defense," said Rose.

Second baseman Joe Morgan, a slip of a man at 5-7 and 155 pounds, batted .351 and was on base 97 times, hit 10 homers and scored the winning run eight times, knocking in the game-winner nine times during the 41-9 explosion. More than any Cincinnati Red, Joe Morgan was relentless.

Johnny Bench, though taking periodic cortisone shots in an ouchy shoulder that was to bother him all season, ignited 12 homers and knocked in 47 runs, with seven game-winning hits. And, he caught, he played first base, he played left field, and he played right field. Bench's shoulder was injured on April 22 in a home plate collision with San Francisco's Gary Matthews.

George Foster, a 190-pound man with a 32-inch waist, celebrated his release from a seemingly life sentence in the dugout, smashing nine home runs, batting .308 and was the owner of four game-winning hits during the 50-game miracle.

Starting pitchers Jack Billingham, Don Gullett and Clay Kirby were 17-0 and relief pitcher Will McEnaney helped them with a 1.15 earned run average in 38 2/3s innings during the 50 games.

The relentless Reds faltered a bit after the All-Star break, losing five of seven, but soon righted themselves and by the end of July they were 32 games over .500 and the Dodgers were so far behind, 14½

games, several Reds took delight after each of those endless victories in asking, "What did the Dodgers do tonight?"

And, more than anything, it was Pete Rose's switch to third base that ignited the Big Red Machine.

It wasn't the first time Rose moved to third base. When he became a Big Red Machinist in 1963, Pete was a second baseman. In 1966, nine years ago, Rose was moved from second to third in spring training. Rose was livid about it then. Charlie Hustle became uncharacteristically sad, sullen and morose. Playing third base was a cursed event. He hated it. Eventually, then manager Don Heffner moved him back to second.

So why was Rose so content to try it again, nine years later?

"The big difference was that Sparky Anderson didn't tell me I was going to third base, he asked if I'd consider it," Rose said. "I told him I thought I'd give it a try if it would help the team."

When Heffner became manager in 1966, Rose wasn't consulted, he was ordered to shift from second to third. Heffner had told writers about the switch over the winter before telling Rose.

"I wasn't quite 25 and I'd just come off the biggest year of my life . . . my first .300 year (.312), my first 200-hit year (209) and my biggest run production season (81)." And, the National League players voted him the All-Star second baseman.

During one spring training game, Rose botched two double play grounders against Detroit. In the clubhouse, Rose erupted: "I'm not doin' nothin' right, nothin' by instinct," he snorted. "Instead of goin' ahead and makin' the play, I'm thinkin' about it first. I'm even missin' pop flies. I'm disgusted."

Heffner persisted, leaving Rose dangling at third as the season began, until finally upon the 16th game, Rose moved back to second base. In July, Don Heffner was fired.

A year later, new Manager Dave Bristol moved Rose to the outfield, and that's where he stayed until the night of May 3, 1975.

Anderson confesses he toyed with the idea of putting Rose at third during spring training this season, but didn't want to upset him. "I got to thinking more and more about it after the season opened, trying to get more punch in the lineup since we weren't getting any offense at all from the guys playing third," Sparky said.

Finally, the opportunity arrived, but Anderson made it clear: "If this bothers you in any way, I'll make this deal with you, Pete. You tell me you don't want to play third and I'll put you back in the outfield." Later, Anderson shook his head and said, "My mistake was not doing it in the spring. He's a full-fledged third baseman." And, Rose was unbelievably happy. "It's fun," he said. "I'm in the game. I carry on a running conversation with the pitcher. I'm having a ball."

And, the Reds had a ball.

They were in the midst of an incredible season. The numbers are mind-boggling. In 45 of their 108 victories, the opposing teams scored

first, but the Reds came from behind to win. In 23 games, the Reds won on their last turn at bat, an unbelievable statistic. Their record in one-run games was 33-20. They were 11-4 in extra-inning games. And, at home, they were invincible, 62 wins, 19 losses - - and they never lost a Saturday game in Riverfront stadium.

The Houston Astros can attest to Cincinnati's penchant for teasing foes, then jerking away victories.

On June 21, the Reds and Astros battled into the tenth inning tied, 4-4. In the top of the 10th, Bob Watson doubled in two runs for a 6-4 lead. In Cincinnati's 10th, Tony Perez homered and Cesar Geronimo singled. With two outs, George Foster doubled, tying the game, 6-6. The Reds won in the 14th when, with two outs and nobody on, pitcher Fred Norman singled, took third on Rose's double and scored on Ken Griffey's single for a 7-6 victory. Joe Niekro was the losing pitcher.

On June 30, Houston's Bob Watson homered with a man aboard in the seventh to give his team a 6-2 lead. In Cincinnati's eighth, Ken Griffey's bases-loaded triple sliced it to 6-5. In the ninth, Dan Driessen singled, Tony Perez doubled and pinch-hitter Bill Plummer hit a sacrifice fly to tie it, 6-6, and send it into extra innings. In the 12th, with two outs, Griffey doubled, Joe Morgan was walked intentionally and John Bench bombed one over the left field wall for a 9-6 success. Joe Niekro was the losing pitcher.

On July 1, the next day, Houston took a 7-4 lead into the ninth. An error, three walks, Cesar Geronimo's double and two sacrifice flies against the by-now jittery Astros tied it, 7-7. The game stretched to four-and-a-half hours until the 15th inning when Pete Rose walked, Ken Griffey singled and Joe Morgan singled for an 8-7 victory. Joe Niekro was the losing pitcher.

The next day, the third and final game of the series, Joe Niekro walked into the Houston clubhouse before the game and said, "Here I am, ready to sweep the series." The Reds won that one, 4-3, on George Foster's three-run sixth-inning homer after Houston scored three in the first. Joe Niekro was NOT the losing pitcher.

That's the way it went all season for The Big Red Machine, relentlessly plodding on, never conceding defeat until the last pitch thudded into a fielder's glove.

By Game 162, the last of the long, long season, the Reds were 19 games beyond reach of the Dodgers. You'd think they would be content to play out the season lethargically. They did have a bit of a lull in mid-September.

But, now it was September 28 and the Atlanta Braves were in town with 44,130 fans seated in Riverfront. The Reds scored thrice in the first but Atlanta plastered Fred Norman and grabbed a 5-3 lead going into the eighth. The Machine slammed five hits, including a two-run double by Cesar Geronimo and a single by Pete Rose that gave Cincinnati a 6-5 lead as the ninth began.

With many of the fans streaming out, Atlanta's Dave May propelled a Will McEnaney fast ball over the right field fence with one out in the ninth, tying it, 6-6, and setting it up one more time for The Come From Behind Gang - - The Relentless Reds. Tony Perez struck out, but Bill Plummer reached when third baseman Darrell Evans threw away his ground ball. Plummer trotted to second on a passed ball, reached third on a fielder's choice and scored on Geronimo's high-bouncing infield hit to shortstop . . . 7-6.

The Cincinnati Reds ended the season, their 108th victory an apropos example of what they had done all year.

GRIFF STORMS HOME -- Ken Griffey slides home to score for the Reds during a regular season contest at Riverfront Stadium. Ken scored 95 runs during 1975.

SPEED AND POWER -- Dave Concepcion, who gets a longer lead off first than any other runner in the National League, jumps back to the bag (above); George Foster flexes the batting muscles that carried him to a .300 season in '75.

THE RED MACHINE IN FULL GEAR -- Joe Morgan dives for a grounder at Riverfront; on page 17, Pete Rose hustles home against the Montreal Expos in bottom shot; above, Merv Rettenmund ducks back from an inside pitch and Rawly Eastwick displays his pitching form.

PAT DARCY

chapter two

The door to George "Sparky" Anderson's office is locked. And bolted. Inside, in the privacy of his inner sanctum, the man's guts are as tautly-strung as a tennis racquet. It is two days before the 1975 World Series and what could be a magnificent personal triumph for the 41-year-old manager of the Cincinnati Reds.

Forty-one years old. His hair is bond-paper white. A few years ago, Anderson traveled with black dye tucked in his dop kit, keeping his locks dark and his appearance youthful enough to match his birth certificate's age. But, in the last couple of years, he lowered his vanity and permitted his hair to go its natural way, wedding-gown white.

As do many men in his precarious profession, Anderson saturates an ulcer with milk. His dark, always-tanned face, carries many worry lines, deepened from many hours under mid-day sun rays from sleeping next to hotel-motel swimming pools on the road, awaiting the endless procession of night games.

Since the day Reds' President Robert L. Howsam rescued Anderson from the coaching staff of the San Diego Padres, from whence he was not exactly met by the Welcome Wagon in Cincinnati, Anderson has kept an "Open Door Policy" to his office. On the inside of his office door is a plaque that rhapsodizes about the merits of a smile - - how easy it is to give one, without cost to the donor.

Today, though, Thursday, October 10, 1975, the door is closed and the only person who can read the smile sign is Anderson, from inside.

Finally, the door opens and Sparky reluctantly admits a half-dozen newsmen. He is seated behind his desk, a half-cup of black coffee sitting cold near his arm as he rips open letters.

"Ask 'em quick, men," he snaps uncharacteristically. "I gotta lot of work to do. I'll keep working, you keep asking." Normally, a writer is as welcome in Sparky's office as his petite, introverted wife, Carol. A newsman walks in and Anderson greets him by name and asks him, "How's the family?" or "What can I do for you, Bobby?"

Not this day. He seems as if he is hanging on the precipice, a man on the ragged edge. Maybe he is. Before the 1974 season, Anderson told the world the Cincinnati Reds would, "Win it all, I promise you."

Not only did the Reds not "win it all," they didn't even win the National League's Western Division, finishing a wobbly second to the Los

Angeles Dodgers. And, the season before, after taking the National League West, the Reds were stunned in the National League Playoffs by the New York (Ya Gotta Believe) Mets.

The Reds won pennants in 1970 and 1972, but lost the World Series to Baltimore and Oakland. Cincinnati's fans, 2,315,603 of them paying their way into antiseptic Riverfront stadium, were getting restless in 1975. The whispers were becoming shouts, "The Reds can't win the big games."

Anderson, of course, heard them. Every night, when he trudged to the pitching mound to tell his pitcher his night was over, he heard them. Even though the Reds wrecked the National League West in 1975, burying the Dodgers by 20 games, Anderson heard the boos. Then, the Big Red Machine thundered past the Pittsburgh Pirates in three straight during the National League Playoffs for its third pennant in five years. But, a World Series championship had eluded them.

"I can afford to buy diamonds," said Captain Pete Rose. "But the only real diamond I want is the one that comes in that World Series ring. I want to get one, have my ears pierced, and dangle that ring from my right ear so the world can see it."

Now, the American League's Boston Red Sox were standing in Cincinnati's way, the upstart darlings of the nation, surprise American League winners, a young team with nothing to lose. The Big Red Machine was EXPECTED to flatten them in four straight. Is it possible to win a World Series in three straight?

Perhaps that's why George "Sparky" Anderson was snippy with the local

HUNCH IN GAME TWO -- "I'm pitching (Jack) Billingham because he pitched well in the 1972 World Series," Sparky Anderson told the press.

FURROWED BROW -- "I'm not that deep of a thinker," Sparky Anderson insisted when questioned about the reasoning behind his pitching moves.

writers as The Machine oiled up. Pressure. Win the big game. Show the world.

People in Cincinnati weren't concerned with the Boston Red Sox. Nope. They were worried about The Green Monster in Boston's Fenway Park - - that 37-foot high left field wall, a cement block and tin demon that sits only 315 feet down the line, so close that shortstops fear bumping their butts when they bend over to field ground balls.

Asked about it this day, Sparky responds, "I won't think about it till we get there. I hear it's not that tricky. We'll work on it tomorrow."

Earlier, Sparky announced that tall right hander Jack Billingham, Cactus Jack, would start Sunday's second game after Don Gullett pitched the opener. Billingham stumbled through September like an automaton set for self-destruction. Guys who didn't get base hits got hit by Billingham with pitches.

The writers wanted to know why Billingham instead of right hander Pat Darcy, a curly-haired rookie who had been pitching well. "I don't know . . . I really don't know," Sparky responded. I'm not that deep of a thinker. I'm pitching Billingham because he pitched well in the 1972 World Series." The newsmen looked at one another, but dutifully jotted it down.

Adding to Sparky's furrowed brow are two unhappy pitchers, Fred Norman and Darcy. Norman, who also pitched well late in the season, started the second Playoff game against Pittsburgh and was stupendous - - six innings of four-hit ball. But, Sparky passed him by, too.

"I thought I helped carry

the club late in the season and earned a World Series start,'' Norman fumed. Earlier, Darcy, winner of 11 games and eight in a row at one time, remarked, ''If Sparky had given me enough starts, I could've won 20 games.''

Anderson is not a well-loved manager by his starting pitchers. Well-respected, yes. Well-loved, no. But, Anderson is not paid to gain love, just victories. The non-love stems from his penchant for yanking starting pitchers at the first sign of distress.

Once this season, the Reds (or Sparky) set a major league record . . . 45 games in a row that a starter did not complete his assignment. Forty-five straight non-complete games on a team that won 108 games. That number, 108 victories, speaks for itself. Still, the pitchers didn't like it.

It was pointed out to Anderson that only one left handed pitcher started and defeated Boston in Fenway Park all season, so why was he starting lefty Don Gullett in the first game.

''Don Gullett is going to be in Baseball's Hall of Fame,'' he said. ''I'd pitch him in Yellowstone Park - - or anywhere.''

Anderson told the writers circling his desk that earlier in the week he left Pittsburgh, after the Playoffs, in a happy mood, but hints of irritation crept into his voice several times during the post-game celebration. Sparky revealed he was dedicating the victory to a paralyzed and gravely-ill California friend.

In the confused and crowded clubhouse, several times different writers asked the man's name and how to spell it. Finally, Sparky half-shouted, ''Milt

Blish! B-l-i-s-h! Milt Blish!'' Then, the telephone rang in his office, somebody wanting Gullett. ''M'am, the guys are awful busy,'' Anderson said. ''Leave a message at the switchboard.'' The woman insisted it was an emergency and Anderson began screaming, ''Gullett, Gullett, Gullett!'' When Gullett didn't respond, Anderson screamed at equipment manager Bernie Stowe to chase him down. Yelling at Stowe was also highly uncharacteristic of Anderson.

The next morning, Anderson received a telephone call asking him about a report in a Boston newspaper that he had sent film of Red Sox pitcher Luis Tiant to the league office, showing that Tiant was balking on his delivery. Anderson maintained he never did it, or even said he did it.

''We win the playoffs and

THE BIG MOTION -- Don Gullett gives it the full extension as he whips the ball home. He fanned 98 batters during the '75 regular season.

DRAWING BACK -- *Just before the season ended, Sparky warned a few regular writers traveling with the Reds that he was going to be awfully quiet during the World Series and Playoffs!*

them out and shoot them, too,'' Sparky answered.

Sparky, nearly always accessible to writers and quick to answer every question directly and honestly, threatened, ''I know what's happening. I can feel it happening, I feel it coming. I'm drawing back, drawing back. If I draw completely back, writers are going to lose a good story-teller. That's a damn shame.''

Just before the season ended, Sparky warned a few regular writers traveling with the Reds, ''I'm going to be awfully quiet during the World Series and Playoffs. I know there are a few writers hanging back, waiting for just that one little quote. Then, they jump all over you with both feet.''

Anderson retreated in his personal time machine five years, to the 1970 World Series, for an example. ''There were several writers jammed around me,'' he said. ''My quote was, 'Frank Robinson is having a tough time seeing in the twilight.' It came out that I said, 'Frank Robinson is in the twilight of his career.' There's a helluva difference, isn't there?''

Just a few days before this unusual by-play with writers in his pre-World Series office chat, Anderson let another personal occurrence creep from his compact, trim body.

By order of management, no reasons given - - it IS an order - - the Cincinnati Reds are permitted no beards and no mustaches. The sideburns must not slip below the ear and hair must not creep over collars. There are no high-cut stirrups on the baseball socks of the Cincinnati Reds. Conformity is godliness. No exceptions.

Well, there was one exception in the family of George ''Sparky'' Anderson.

I'm happy,'' Anderson said. ''The next morning I find out about the Tiant thing. It's not fair to me, my family, my ball club. It's a total lie . . . and if this keeps up, I'm going to stop everything.'' Stop everything?

''If this keeps up, my door will be closed to everybody,'' Anderson continued. ''The truth is going to start coming out or everything will stop. If this is what the writing business is coming to, they ought to take 'em all out and shoot 'em.''

Cincinnati columnist Tom Callahan, a visitor in Sparky's office this day before the World Series began, replied, ''Managers aren't totally honest. I've been lied to by managers.''

''Then, they should take

Not his baseball family. It was his 15-year-old son, Lee. The battle lasted two years.

"His hair was so long it was tied in a pony-tail," Sparky revealed after Cincinnati's Playoff championship. "I had told him and told him to get it cut before I came home after the baseball season. When I came home, it was still hanging down in a pony-tail. Lee was in the garage working on his motor-bike, bent over it on his knees.

"I demanded that he get it cut. I told him as long as I was buying his clothes and his food, he would do as I said while he was living under my roof."

Lee said no, continuing his tinkering on the bike. Anderson realized that his son was going to be as stubborn as the ol' man.

"The only way for me to get him to cut his hair was to get down and whip him with my bare hands," Sparky added. "I didn't want to fight my own kid, so I just walked off and left him flat. I cut him off from me, my own kid. I had nothing to do with him for a year. He talked to his mother but I lost him. He wouldn't talk to me at all."

If you ask Sparky about his "no long hair policy" with the Reds, he'll give you a free lecture about the adherent dangers - - marijuana, atheism, uncleanliness, lack of discipline, no self-respect.

When the Reds headed West in April, Sparky detoured home to Thousand Oaks, Calif., and Lee still wore the long locks. "Lee and I had a real knockdown, dragout fight," Anderson admitted to Louisville columnist Dave Kindred.

"We both learned something from it," Anderson admitted. "Lee woke up to the things I was saying and I awoke to him.

My wife said to me, 'If your son committed a murder, would you stand by him?' I would, of course. I'd be there every day, standing beside him. And she said, 'Then why don't you stand behind him in this? Give him your love.'"

Anderson was not ashamed to admit he was wrong in the handling of Lee and said he realized something else is more important than short hair and creased pants. "Love is more important," he admits. "I'd always hid my feelings. The success of the ball club this year might have something to do with me opening up. I have security and I have confidence.

"I was trying to protect my own image," he added. "There was Lee with his long hair and I was there with my short hair image. I'm ashamed of myself. I was being the child and Lee the man."

After the Pirates were dispatched, Lee waited for Sparky at the airport and kissed him on the lips. "I wouldn't show any affection before. We're together now. All he wanted was a little affection."

Peace and tranquility with Lee didn't mean all the barriers were lowered for the Cincinnati Reds. The hair stays short, the sideburns stay high and the socks stay low. Sparky is convinced the Cincinnati Reds represent the conservative Midwest. Some of the team's popularity is traced to its clean-cut, well-scrubbed, predictable athletes, he believes.

Sometimes that attitude is difficult to dispute. Where else could a baseball franchise offer a Farm Night and have 40,000 fans show up, all hopeful of winning a tractor, pickup truck or cow in a post-game drawing?

Maybe the team does reflect the attitudes of its citizens. The "conform or else" dictum comes from the top through club president Bob Howsam and his assistant Dick Wagner. Individuality is discouraged, except as a means to use one's talents to win baseball games for The Cincinnati Reds, Inc. As a result, the only thing colorful about the Reds is the red trimming on their uniforms.

Once, Pete Rose had difficulty locating his plastic batting helmet so he chalked a very small "14" on the back of it. The game was on TV back in Cincinnati and the brass spotted it during a closeup. A call to the clubhouse followed and by the time Rose came to bat again, the "14" had magically disappeared.

There is a certain brand of baseball shoe that comes with white stripes on the side and another brand with a white wing. Both brands, with their distinguishing trademarks, are highly visible on other teams. Not the Cincinnati Reds. When the new shoes arrive, a clubhouse boy busily brushes black shoe polish over the white trademarks so all the shoes are alike in appearance.

On other clubs, when there are two outs and the catcher is on deck, he usually wears his shin guards in the on deck circle just in case the hitter makes the third out. The catcher can then slip on his chest protector and be ready to catch. It saves time. Not the Cincinnati Reds. John Bench and Bill Plummer never wear the shin guards to the on deck circle. Always think optimistically, decrees management. The hitter is not going to make that third out.

No matter where the Reds go, people want to know why . . . why do the Reds lead the league in short hair cuts? Sparky patiently explains, time and again.

"If a player has pride enough to do all these things we ask of him, he has pride enough to do all the things we ask of him on the field," he says. "We stress discipline from the first day a kid comes into our organization, right down in the lowest minors. Discipline isn't always screaming and hollering. Discipline is also love (Where have we heard that?). I never scream at our veterans. Once in a while I do to some of the kids. Most of us are veterans and I get more accomplished by sitting down and discussing - - get their views, too," Anderson says.

"Just because I'm a manager and they are players doesn't make me no smarter than them," he says, as usual, brutalizing proper English. Anderson's constant use of poor language concerned his wife, Carol, and she used to make him sit at the kitchen table studying grammar books. Sparky didn't want to fight it and Carol gave up. The way he says something isn't as important as his sincerity, which is seldom questioned.

"I didn't get smarter about baseball from the day I quit playing until the day I became a coach," Anderson added. "And, I didn't get no smarter the day I left coaching and became a manager."

There is another tenet adhered to by a Cincinnati Red. No hanging heads after defeat. "That's pride," Anderson explains. "We don't sit around and cry when we lose. We give it our best shot for two-and-a-half hours on the field. To me, if I see a guy hanging his head after a loss, it means he is ashamed because he didn't give his best for two-and-a-half hours between the white lines."

So, that's the Cincinnati Philosopy. Love it or hate it, to wear the red and white double-knits of the Cincinnati Reds, Inc., you best abide. If not, you might quickly find yourself growing a beard, mustache and long hair in a different colored uniform.

Relief pitcher Pedro Borbon, a Dominican who raises fighting cocks, is Anderson's designated barber. Borbon spends many moments in the clubhouse trimming neck-lines and hair protruding over ears.

Borbon packed his scissors, Anderson packed up his troubled, worried, pressured mind and the Cincinnati Reds headed for Boston and the World Series.

MAN WITH THE CLIPPERS -- Fireman Pedro Borbon is occasionally pressed into service as a clubhouse barber. If Sparky spots a shaggy neck-line or extra hair over the ears, Borbon and his scissors are called upon.

SERIES MOVES TO BOSTON -- clockwise from bottom, the cornerstone plaque at Fenway tells the history of the park; Tony Perez takes a swat at the famous left field wall in batting practice; the two managers, Darrell Johnson (left) and Sparky Anderson [right], compare notes.

HURLER'S HUDDLE --
Jack Billingham (left)
and Bill Lee (right) the
starting pitchers in
game two of the Series,
talk things over during
the workouts in photo on
right; below, Don Gullett
delivers a pitch in Series
game one.

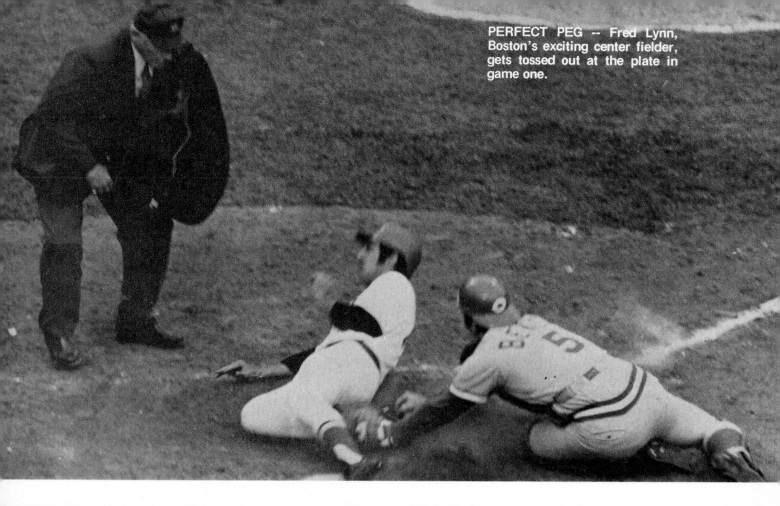

PERFECT PEG -- Fred Lynn, Boston's exciting center fielder, gets tossed out at the plate in game one.

chapter three

The Cincinnati Reds arrived in Boston via American Airlines chartered Boeing 707 on Friday morning, October 11, 1975 and were immediately transported to the Statler-Hilton hotel near the Common.

Travel arrangements are made by traveling secretary Paul Campbell, a lovable ex-major league first baseman with a penchant for ice cream and long walks . . . to get rid of the ice cream's calories. Campbell performs his duties meritoriously and is one year away from retirement. ''So many of my friends I played ball with are dying I'm afraid to look in the obituaries. I might see my name,'' Campbell said one day last season while tossing aside a newspaper in a hotel lobby.

As traveling secretary, Campbell catches all the flak from the players when things aren't perfect. And,

with ball players, things aren't often perfect. They certainly weren't at the Statler-Hilton, though it wasn't Campbell's fault. Available rooms in Boston were rare. The available rooms in the Statler-Hilton were clean, but rather small. Rather.

After visiting his room, Pete Rose stepped into the hotel elevator, populated by five other passengers and said, ''Damn, what's everybody doing in my room?''

Pitcher Clay Kirby was aboard the elevator and resurrected a line he used when the Reds checked into the Sheraton-Mount Royal for the first time this season. ''My room is so small, I have to leave it to change my mind.''

Shoulder miseries and bad pitch-itis bothered Kirby most of 1975 and by World Series time most people had forgotten what uniform

number Kirby wore. The last half of the season, he pitched hardly at all. That didn't stop him from being optimistic when the hassles developed in the pitching staff over who should and who shouldn't be pitching. ''I should start a World Series game,'' Kirby said with a grin. ''It's been so long since I pitched there's no way Boston could have a scouting report on me.''

Shortly after checking in, the Reds gathered in the lobby for a trip to Fenway Park and their first glimpse of The Green Monster, lurking in the left field corner awaiting their arrival, probably with a lecherous grin. If The Monster were a living organism, it would present one hell of a strike zone. Fortunately for visiting teams, The Green Monster is not The Jolly Green Giant turned vicious. It's just a wall, a wall standing there doing a grand imitation of the Grand Cooley dam. But, for a week, the Reds talked as if they were playing handball against the Wall, instead of baseball against the Bosox.

The only Reds with Wall experience are ex-Orioles Merv Rettenmund and Terry Crowley, two extra players who suddenly became centers-of-attention when writers sought them out for Wall quotes.

"The upper half of the wall is tin," Rettenmund explains. "The ball hits the tin and falls straight down. The lower half is concrete block. If the ball hits that, it comes back at you like a rocket. And, the scoreboard has so many nooks and crevices that when a ball hits in it, you don't know which way the ball might bounce.

"The closeness of the wall enables Boston left fielder Carl Yastrzemski to play shallow out there," Rettenmund continues. "He catches a lot of line drives that normally would fall in front of an outfielder in other parks. The thing we'll have to watch is that you must be careful trying to score from second on a base-hit to left and you must be careful trying to get a double on a drive off the wall. You can easily be thrown out at second." The Reds were to discover that, painfully, more than once during the Series.

As the yellow city bus picked its way through Boston's wretched but picturesque streets toward Fenway, Rose offered his views on what was about to happen.

"Wall, wall, wall," he said. "We ain't worried about no wall. We're gonna bunt and steal 'em. They can talk all they want about walls, but they ain't seen nothin' like Don Gullett."

YAZ IN LEFT -- Merv Rettenmund describes how the Red Sox left fielder handles his job: "The closeness of the wall enables Boston left fielder Carl Yastrzemski to play shallow out there. He catches a lot of line drives that normally would fall in front of an outfielder in other parks."

Mr. and Mrs. Bob Howsam and Mr. and Mrs. Louis Nippert cheer the Reds on.

MORGAN'S FIRST IMPRESSION OF FENWAY -- "Joe Morgan cast a glance around the one-tiered 33,379-seat stadium. 'Looks like a minor league park,' he said. 'And, with all the pillars, a guy could kill himself in the stands trying to find his seat.'"

The bus disgorged the Reds at Fenway's press entrance behind home plate. The Reds disembarked and headed up a ramp that opened in a portal directly behind home plate. One-by-one they stopped as they reached the portal and could view the field, each one's head immediately turning left for a breath-taking view of The Wall.

"Wow, you can reach out and touch it from here," said left fielder George Foster, the man who must play out there, standing at the foot of Mount Green Monster. Then, Foster began tip-toeing in its direction, as if sneaking up on it. "Shhh," Foster said, putting a finger to his lips. "Don't wake him up."

Foster stopped and pointed. "Ah, ha. I see a solution. See that ladder running up the wall from the top of the scoreboard to the netting above the wall. If they give me a rope to climb up to that ladder. I can scale that thing and catch me a few fly balls."

Joe Morgan cast a glance around the one-tiered 33,379-seat stadium. "Looks like a minor league park," he said. "And, with all the pillars, a guy could kill himself in the stands trying to find his seat." Said Rose, "Nice little ball park they have here. Nice . . . and little."

Boston coach Don Zimmer was on the field, hitting fungoes to the Red Sox when the Reds came in. Zimmer knows all about the Reds. He played for them and he managed against them at San Diego, when San Diego was the leper colony of baseball. "I think," said Zimmer, drilling a line drive off the tin heart of The Wall, "the Reds should forget about The Wall." Then, he grinned.

Foster offered the best

31

advice. "If our pitchers throw no-hitters, we won't have to worry at all about The Wall." The last no-hitter in Fenway Park was perpetrated by Dave Morehead against Cleveland in 1965.

The Reds dressed and began taking batting practice. Former Cincinnati pitcher Brooks Lawrence was throwing and Johnny Bench began smashing pitch after pitch over the 37-foot-high demon, some landing in the screen above the wall and some peppering buildings beyond the stadium across Lansdowne Street. At one point, Bench orbited five straight over the looming giant. After the fifth one, he yelled to Lawrence, "Forget about The Wall, Brooks," Bench's statement was a sarcastic reminder of its presence. A couple of his batting practice homers were off his bat handle, another came on a half-swing off the bat's end.

Immediately after stepping out of the batting cage, one of those guys from Instant-3, Total-11 or Scenic-8 shoved a microphone in front of Bench and said, "I noticed you seem to be trying to pull everything. Is that the influence of The Wall?"

"No, I'm a pull hitter," Bench patiently explains. "I'm pulling the ball all the time, any park, even if it's Yosemite." At least, he didn't say Yellowstone.

After the workout, Anderson was swallowing some coffee in his Fenway office and said, "A lot of people aren't going to like to hear this," he began. "I don't plan to change a thing during the Series. I plan to manage exactly the way I managed during the season.

I've spent a lot of time worrying about it and talking to myself," he admitted. "Don't change a thing you've been doing."

Having seen Fenway and chatting with writers, Anderson seemed himself again, gregarious and smiling easily. But his admission that he was giving himself pep talks about not changing his managerial methods revealed that the pressure beneath the surface was still there.

Anderson's method for winning 108 regular season games and three National League Playoff games was ample use of the bullpen, a bullpen populated by a pleasant blend of youth and experience.

In 162 games, Sparky had permitted his starters to complete only 22 games - - eight by Don Gullett, who

GOTCHA! -- Rick Burleson's stolen base attempt in the first game of the Series was foiled as Dave Concepcion took Johnny Bench's throw and tagged Burleson out.

missed two months with a fractured pitching thumb. Jack Billingham and Gary Nolan completed five, Fred Norman two, Clay Kirby one and Pat Darcy one. Darcy's one was the game that stopped Cincinnati's streak at 45 without a complete game.

For the past few seasons, Cincinnati's bullpen stars have been 34-year-old Clay Carroll and 29-year-old Pedro Borbon. And, they contributed again. Borbon was 9-5 with five saves and Carroll was 7-5 with seven saves.

But, the heavy, important work was done by a pair of unproven rookies - - unproven until 1975. Will McEnaney, a flakey left hander and only 23, was 5-2 with 15 saves. Rawlins Jackson Eastwick III, a studious right hander and only 24, was 5-3 with 22 saves. McEnaney and Eastwick were usually the last ones in a game, dictated by whether Sparky wanted a right hander or left hander working.

"The way Sparky keeps coming out of the dugout waving pitchers in and out, other teams must think we have 35 men on our roster," Rose said. There have been games when it seemed as if 35 relief pitchers were in and out of the game, all wearing Cincinnati uniforms. The quickness with which Captain Hook Anderson jerks them in and out of the lineup is the source of clubhouse humor among other players, and slight resentment among the four relief pitchers, all highly-competitive and cocky enough to believe they can do the job themself.

"There is no question that relief pitchers don't like the way Sparky runs the staff," says pitching coach Larry Shepard. "But they do what they are asked and they do it

well. They're the best."

McEnaney, an outspoken young lad who talks even louder with his left arm, comes right out and says it. "There have been times when Sparky took me out when I thought I could have stayed in and got the next man out. But, I don't say anything. He's been around a lot longer than I have. I don't think Sparky plays any favorites, though. If he did, I probably would never pitch. I don't think the man likes me personally."

When confronted with McEnaney's words, Sparky grinned and replied, "I don't ever get close to a rookie. They might not be around too long. I don't let them know how I feel. But, McEnaney will be around a while. He's feisty and has a lot of get up and go."

If Anderson shows any favoritism, it is toward Eastwick. Sparky likes his self-confidence, his cockiness - - and his fast ball. Asked if he ever thought about walking

Pitching coach Larry Shepard offers tips to fireman Will McEnaney on his delivery.

halfway toward home plate, then stopping and shouting at the hitter, "I'm gonna get you out . . . no way you could get a hit off me," Eastwick said, "I'm not John (The Count) Montefusco. I just think it to myself."

There were many games during which Anderson used all four in a game. After one, during which the four guys saved Gullett a 3-2 victory over St. Louis, shortstop Dave Concepcion chided Anderson with, "You've done it before, and you'll do it again. You've hooked 'em all." There was raucous laughter in the clubhouse and Anderson replied with a wide smile.

Joe Morgan offered a suggestion to the relief pitchers. "You guys should hide in the bullpen so Sparky can't find you. The one he doesn't find until last might finish the game and get the save or victory."

Rawlins Jackson Eastwick III is a name guaranteeing any kid instant sissification. His life should be directed toward chemistry books, model airplanes and finding ways to duck gym classes. Rawly could have been Robert or Ralph or Richard. Robert and Richard are his older twin brothers. Ralph is his identical twin brother, 15 minutes older.

"My parents were hung up with the letter R," Eastwick says. "They weren't expecting another set of twins. Since I was last out of the chute, they gave me my father's name."

Rawlins Jackson Eastwick III went through life fighting about his name, like Johnny Cash's "Boy Named Sue." With two older brothers and a brother the same age, Rawly knew how to fight. Cracked plaster and broken windows were badges of valor at the Eastwick house in Haddonfield, N.J. "I was sick of school from the first

PROUD FIGHTER "Rawlins Jackson Eastwick, III went through life fighting about his name..."

day of kindergarten," Eastwick said. "By the time I was 16, I was attending summer baseball camps. College was not for me, I'm not the college type."

Don't believe that blatant lie. If there is a "college type" on the roster of the Cincinnati Reds, Rawlins Jackson Eastwick III is the one. He is a collector of antique jewelry, he is a painter (artist, not house) and a deep thinker." Mainly, R. J. Eastwick is the best relief pitcher the Reds own -- maybe in baseball? Would you believe it? Well, Rawly believes it, and it's most important that he believes it.

Outspoken is another Eastwick trait. He admitted just before the start of the World Series that he thought about the Most Valuable Player award. "Sure, I've thought about MVP," he said. "But, more than anybody else, that belongs to Joe Morgan. I think I've done more for my team than any other rookie in the league. So, I've thought about Rookie of the Year, too."

Eastwick admits his unusual name helped when he joined the Reds from Indianapolis on May 18 when Anderson sent him there after spring training. "I hated the name as a kid, but my name set things up for me when I first came up," he said. "I mean, people wanted to know who, in baseball, could be named Rawlins Jackson Eastwick III? It put my foot in the door. I was interviewed on TV because of it and people thought it was funny to yell my name mockingly from the stands. Now I'm known because of what I've accomplished. I think I've earned it."

Eastwick, like Borbon, is eccentric about his right arm. Nobody touches that golden arm without permission, and permission seldom is granted. The training room is like Folsom prison; Rawly wants to visit only for educational purposes. No rubdowns, no ice packs, no foul-smelling liniments or ointments.

"The best thing for my arm is to leave it alone," he says. "My muscles are supple. I'm long and sinewy, always loose. I don't need that junk. As long as I pitch often, I don't have stiffness. I stay out of the training room."

Eastwick's proudest possession, other than a moving fast ball, is a $200 Persian turquoise money clip. He also owns a $500 gold ring with 21 sapphires that is more than 100 years old. At the easel, Rawly calls himself an "expressionist." "I experiment a lot . . . I just sit at the canvas and interpret things I create in my mind. I haven't sold anything, but the best thing I've done is an interpretation of a vase, jug and basket of fruit. I gave it to Johnny and Vickie Bench as a wedding gift. They were impressed with it. Something personal means more as a gift."

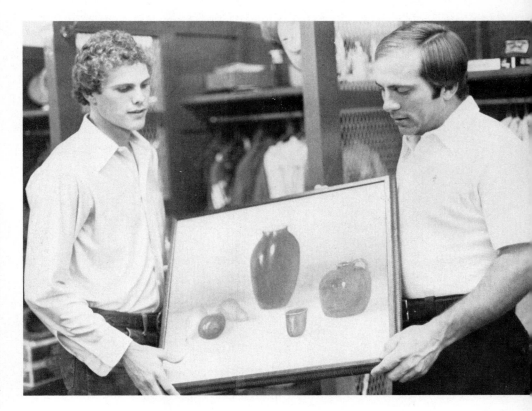

WEDDING GIFT -- Rawly Eastwick presents one of his paintings to Johnny Bench as a wedding present.

THE HAWK

Rawly takes no razzing from the he-men types that populate the Cincinnati roster. Perhaps it is because Eastwick believes his "expressionist" attitude carries to the mound. While he is striking out a dangerous hitter to end a game, he is putting the Reds closer to a huge pay-day and vindication.

"Just as I concentrate in front of an easel, I concentrate on the mound," he says. "It's weird. I don't hear the crowd. I know sometimes they are going crazy. It is as if I'm in a vacuum. I see the catcher's glove, that's all. I don't even see the hitter or the umpire. I concentrate so hard, sometimes I get ready to pitch without realizing the umpire isn't behind the plate yet. Pitching is as much using your mental capabilities as your physical capacities.

"Mental concentration takes as much out of you as physical exertion," he adds. Still believe he isn't a college type? Eastwick insists he has never been nervous in his life, swearing he won't become unglued when, or if, he ever gets married. He has one quirk, though. He hates elevators; he is claustrophobic. "When the door closes, I want to start shoving people."

Eastwick and McEnaney are rarities. They are not former starters converted into relief pitchers. They were groomed in Cincinnati's minor league system as relief pitchers.

While working his way through the minor league system, Eastwick admits he once rooted against his own teammates at Three Rivers, Canada in the Eastern League. "I'd go to the ball park and say, 'OK, starting pitcher, go out there and mess up so I can get in there.' Eastwick admits it

CAPTAIN HOOK AT WORK -- Sparky carefully observes his pitchers at work, never being afraid to pull them out quickly when the slightest hint of trouble appears.

was a selfish attitude, but in the minor leagues, selfish attitudes are like road maps to the major leagues.

"In the minors, you are trying to show the big club what you can do," Eastwick says. "The only way I could show them what I could do was to get in the game. That meant the starting pitcher had to mess up." Eastwick never let his feelings be known to the starters. "I didn't want one of them waiting for me at the door," he said.

Now, the Reds and Anderson know what he can do and let him do it. On a bright, sunny Saturday in Riverfront stadium this season, the dying Dodgers were trying to stay in the race. Eastwick went for the jugular and severed it. The Reds were leading, 5-3, in the bottom of the ninth with

two outs. Shortstop Dave Concepcion made an error and starter Jack Billingham walked pinch-hitter Jimmy Wynn.

Dodger Manager Walter Alston sent Ken McMullen up to pinch-hit and Anderson called for Eastwick from the bullpen. When Sparky wanted to tell Eastwick he should throw nothing but fast balls up and in, catcher Johnny Bench stopped him. "I convinced Sparky not to say a word to Eastwick," Bench said.

Sparky complied, merely handing Eastwick the baseball, patting him on the rump, and leaving. "What kind of hitter is McMullen, I've never faced him?" Eastwick asked Bench.

"He is a middle-and-in fast ball hitter," said Bench. "But, he can't hit YOUR fast ball."

Eastwick proved Bench right. Rawly fired three successive fast balls and McMullen, the fast ball hitter, swung futilely at all three, touching nary a one. Game, set, match, Reds.

"I don't like to mess around when I get two strikes on a hitter," Eastwick explains. "Why waste a pitch? When I get a guy 0-and-2, I just think, 'Here it is, you jerk, try to hit it.'" It was the same method he used a week earlier in New York in an almost identical situation. The Reds led, 2-1, but the Mets had the tying and winning runs aboard in the ninth. Fast ball hitter Dave Kingman was up, but Eastwick thundered three express trains past him.

"I feel absolutely no pressure. I'm just having fun playing this game. To me, it's just like out on the sandlots with my twin brothers. I'm like Pete Rose. Have fun and go play. When you think about pressure, that's when you make mistakes," Eastwick said.

"My success is all due to my fast ball, and I don't even know where it's going. It's like a knuckler. Sometimes it sails away, sometimes it slides in, sometimes it goes up and sometimes it drops down." Veteran pitcher Gary Nolan was sitting next to Eastwick in the clubhouse after the Dodger game and said, "Rawly, I had three heart attacks while McMullen was batting, one after each pitch." Then, when Eastwick wasn't listening, Nolan said, "Rawly has two things, poise and self-control. You don't see this very often in somebody this young. He pitches and carries himself like he has been around a lot longer than a few months. I never see him get emotional."

Eastwick's clinical

COMEBACK KID -- Gary Nolan, after almost two years of inactivity, led the Red Staff with 211 innings pitched in 1975.

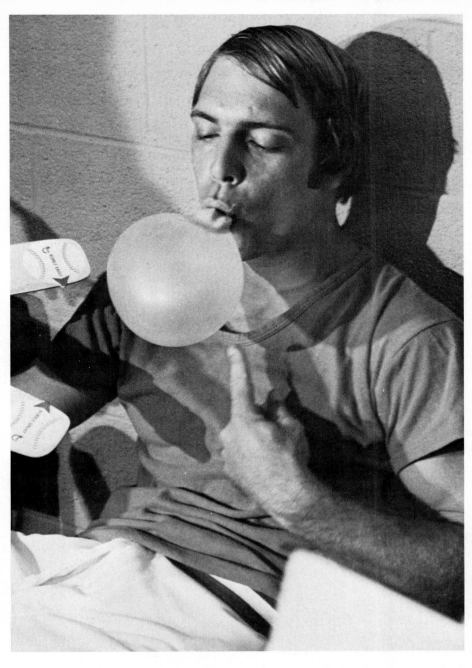

LOOK AT THIS ONE! -- Will McEnaney blows up his entry in a bubble gum contest during the regular season. Despite the size of this bubble, Will didn't win any prizes.

analysis of how to strike out guys like Kingman and McMullen with three straight fast balls in pressure situations is like a surgeon recapping his latest open heart operation.

"I stair-step them," he says. "The first fast ball is around the knees. The second one across the belt. The third one across the letters. At 0-and-2, the pressure is on the hitter. That's why I throw them high fast balls. When a hitter sees a ball up near his eyes, I don't care who he is, it is automatic. He's gotta swing -- gotta go after it. That high one on 0-and-2 is impossible to lay off."

Will McEnaney is ample proof that there is a bit of goofiness in all left handers. Like Eastwick, McEnaney has a twin brother and they thought nothing of switching classes and switching dates, without telling their teachers or their female companions for the evening. Will and his brother are identical, they were never caught by teacher or date.

Once, in fact, Will was so convincing, it took a foreign language to straighten things out at Springfield, Ohio, North high school.

Will was attending a class for his brother one day. There was an important page for McEnaney over the public address system. Will got up to go answer it, but the teacher, thinking Will was his brother, made him sit back down. "The only way we finally got it straightened out," said Will, "was that my brother was taking German and I wasn't. They called him to the office and he spoke German for them. Then, they let me out of class to answer the message."

Those kinds of episodes, plus a beer-drinking incident, were enough for high school officials to keep

McEnaney off the school baseball team his senior year. Instead, he played with older guys on a sandlot team, where scout George Zurkaw saw him.

"Hey, I pride myself on being a little bit different," McEnaney says. "The first time George saw me, he said, 'You're just flakey enough to make it to the major leagues.' " George was right, but there was a time in 1973 when McEnaney almost blew it. Cincinnati's Indianapolis Triple-A team was playing in Wichita. McEnaney started and lasted a few pitches past the National Anthem, forcing manager Vern Rapp to yank him.

As the game continued, McEnaney turned into Hurricane Will in the clubhouse. He dismantled two wooden stools, reducing them to kindling. He knocked two screens off dressing cages. He splintered some wooden dressing stalls and set a minor league record for throwing baseball spikes the hardest across a cluttered room.

"Vern was a bit mad when he saw what a mess I made of that clubhouse," McEnaney said. "I thought sure I'd get fined, but he just told me there were other left handed pitchers in the Cincinnati organization who would like to pitch there. I got the message. I had to pay a security deposit every time I went to Wichita after that. And, I decided to curb my temper for fear of hurting my wallet or my physical well-being."

Though he never shows it outwardly, McEnaney says that temper resides deep within his 175-pound body, ready to surface if needed.

On the field, it hasn't been needed. He may be flakey like a left hander, but he is not wild, a stigma many lefties carry with them to the mound. "Control is the reason I've been successful. Hitters know I throw strikes, so they don't take close pitches," he says, after walking only 23 in 91 innings this season. "In a tight game, they'll swing at those close pitches and usually my guys make the big plays behind me. Control and self-confidence, that's me."

And, what does being "a little bit flakey" mean?

Like laughing and giggling on the bus after a defeat. Everybody knows athletes are supposed to put on sober faces and act disgusted after every defeat. "I can't do it," McEnaney says. "We lose a couple of games, so what? I don't like it, I want to win them all. But, a loss is past

PINPOINT CONTROL -- Will McEnaney walked just 23 batters in 91 innings in '75.

SUPER VAN--One of Will McEnaney's favorite pastimes off the field is working on his van.

history. It's not that important, is it? So I smile."

Pranks play a part in McEnaney's life-style, too. A stranger passes and when his back is to McEnaney, Will might say, "Sir, you dropped something." When the guy looks, Will is looking the other way. "Childish? Yes, but fun," Will grins. "The only time I'm serious is when I walk to the mound. Then, I'm totally relaxed. The only thing funny is when pitching coach Larry Shepard walks to the mound and tells me to throw a slider on the outside corner. I nod my head, but hell, I can't do it. I can't control my slider that well. I can keep it low, but I can't throw it to spots."

When McEnaney first met his wife-to-be, Daryl Lynne, he walked up to her and said, "Hi, my name is Will McEnaney. How you like me so far?"

"I don't," she said coldly.

But, she soon liked him. In fact, the couple's first child was born the night before McEnaney and the Reds left for Boston.

McEnaney weighs ten pounds less than he did in 1972. He was 175 pounds and was 14-5 at Tampa in 1971. In 1972, he was 185 and 11-6 - - an OK record but not as good as 1971.

"I wasn't throwing as well, so I thought, hell, it wouldn't hurt to take off the weight. Besides, I couldn't afford a new wardrobe all the time." So, he took off the excess poundage and kept the 1971 clothes, so he could use them to check his weight. Nobody has the heart to tell him about the marvelous invention called bathroom scales, but then it all goes with being flakey.

Every third day when it's his turn to drive, McEnaney arrives at Riverfront in his bronze Chevy van. "I throw Bill Plummer and Darrel Chaney in the back and truck on in to the stadium," he says. "And sometimes I wonder out loud to them what it might be like to be a starting pitcher. Then I think about Dodger Mike Marshall. Hell, relief pitchers make money."

McEnaney was thinking out loud one day about the reports of Marshall's contract, an erroneous report, Marshall says. The story was that Marshall's contract calls for a water bed on the road and free use of a rental car. "I don't need a water bed, a regular bed suits me fine," McEnaney said. "Just so I have someplace to sleep." Then, his baby blue eyes flashing, he added, "But, I wouldn't mind a car."

Clay Carroll is the first guy to admit he was not brought into this world to be a Rhodes Scholar. When "Rhodes Scholar" was mentioned to him once, he remarked, "Rhodes Scholar? Is that somebody going to school to learn how to build roads. We sure coulda used one in Clanton, Alabama. All our roads are dirt."

The Reds enjoy kidding Clay about his intelligence, or lack thereof. But, if they are all so smart, how come Clay Carroll has been a Cincinnati Reds longer than anybody but Pete Rose and Tony Perez? The Hawk, as he calls himself, is in his eighth season as a Cincinnati relief pitcher.

Well, mostly in relief. Of 485 pitching appearances for Cincinnati, 471 were in relief. The 485 is the most of any pitcher in Cincinnati history. The Hawk started two games this season and relieved in 54. Before one of his two starts, pitching coach Larry Shepard walked over and handed him the pitching charts in a black notebook. It was the night before he was to pitch and it is the next night's pitcher's duty to chart pitches.

"Hey, Hawk," said Jack Billingham. "Want me to

MAC'S CLAN-- Will and Lynne McEnaney with their daughter Faith.

explain those symbols to you? It involves a little more than marking X's." The first year Riverfront stadium opened in 1970, Tommy Helms, one of baseball's all-time non-home run hitters, hit the first home run in the new park. The homer barely cleared the left field wall just inside the foul pole.

Before the next day's game, Carroll and another since-departed pitcher, Wayne Granger, sneaked behind the wall and drew a huge "X" with adhesive tape just above the wall where the ball hit on Tommy's homer. When Helms saw that "X" he quickly said, "I know who did that. Clay Carroll left his signature."

Clay Carroll's professional career started in 1961 when the Braves signed him for $1,000. "Made me mad," said Clay. "The guy told me no other team wanted me. Found out later a couple other teams were interested." Carroll took his new-found fortune and bought a second-hand 1954 Ford. "I needed it to drive to spring training," he said. "But I had this little problem."

"I wanted to show the car off to a couple of cousins," he said. "I took it down a dirt road and around a curve. A tree got in the way. Yeah, it was damaged. So damaged it would take a lot of money to fix. I told the garage to keep it and bought me a train ticket to camp. There went half my bonus, my ride to spring training and my fancy car."

Carroll quickly lost the other half of his bonus in Waycross, Georgia, site of the Braves' camp. "Man, that camp was so far back in the swamps, they had to pipe in sunlight," he said. "We were in Waycross for six weeks and the same movie "pitcher" was a-playin' the

BASEBALL SENSE -- Clay Carroll says, "Baseball was my calling. I was too smart to go to college."

whole time.

"Well, I lost the other half of my bonus on pants," he grinned. "They had this high wire fence surrounding the camp with barbed-wire on top. They padlocked the thing at 11 p.m. and if you weren't in by then you got in as best you could. That's how I ripped up all my britches."

The Hawk grew up as a poor bird. A family of 10 lived on $74 a week his father made in the Clanton Cotton Mill. Clay worked there, too, as a kid, crawling under the gins to clean the frames. "It was hotter'n a french fry fresh out of the pan," he said.

Clay played baseball in Chilton County High School and when he was 13 he was playing weekends with and against men's semi-pro

teams. "They built my ego," Carroll said. "They told me how good my stuff was how I oughtta make baseball my career. I watched baseball on television and it was always a dream to me - - how some day I might be on TV pitching to all them guys I was a-watchin'.

Clanton was nice, the Hawk says, "I ain't a-kiddin' ya, they grow world famous peaches, big as softballs . . . and watermelons the size of a cow's head. But baseball was my calling. I was too smart to go to college. Besides, I didn't get me no offers." So when the man dangled $1,000 in front of him, Clay Carroll was off to seek his fame and fortune. "Shucks, I'da played ball for nothin' a-tall."

The Reds obtained him from Atlanta in 1968 and since then he has been on two All-Star teams (1972-73) and was Fireman of the Year (top relief pitcher) in 1970. "I've stayed with the same team for eight years so I musta done some kinda job, right?" he asks rhetorically.

Carroll is proud and guarded about his profession. When the Reds brought up pitcher Tom Carroll last season, it was decided to put "T. Carroll" on the back of the rookie's uniform and "C. Carroll" on the back of Clay's suit. The rest of the Reds carried only their last names.

Shortly thereafter, the Hawk was in the clubhouse with a needle, removing the Capital C. "Everybody knows who I am," he said. "Look, there are two Clays on this team . . . Clay Carroll and Clay Kirby. There are two Carrolls, Tom Carroll and Clay Carroll. But, there is only ONE Clay Carroll." There is only one Clay Carroll in all of baseball, in name and personality.

With those kinds of divergent people as his relief pitchers, Sparky Anderson was ready to send his Reds against the Boston Red Sox in the 1975 World Series.

THE CARROLL MEN--Clay Carroll and his son Bret pose for a shot in the Red Riverfront Clubhouse.

*DAVEY ON THE STEAL --
Dave Concepcion pilfered 3
bases in the Series.*

PRE-GAME   CONFERENCES--Artist LeRoy Neiman talks with Rawly Eastwick.

Bernie Carbo and Dave
Concepcion exchange
thoughts.

OPPOSING FORCES--The Cincinnati and Boston bullpens are located in right field in Fenway Park.

foes in the series opener.....

TOP PHOTO: Don Gullett had a 15-4 record with a 2.42 ERA during the regular season.

BOTTOM PHOTO: Luis Tiant was 18-14 with a 4.02 ERA during 1975 for the Boston Red Sox.

chapter four

Sparky Anderson and the Cincinnati Reds were ultra-confident when dawn broke over Boston's Back Bay on Saturday, October 11. Lefthander Don Gullett was the scheduled pitcher, a 24-year-old kid who missed two months of the season and still won 15 games, losing only 4.

On June 6, Gullett was 8-3, en route to his ninth victory with two outs in the bottom of the ninth and a 9-2 lead over the Atlanta Braves. He gave up three hits to load the bases and Larvell Blanks was the hitter.

"I toyed with the idea of taking Gullett out," said Anderson. He didn't. Blanks slammed a liner straight back to the mound. Most pitchers would have watched it zing into center field, a two-run single.

Not Don Gullett. Not Don Gullett, the athlete. Gully stuck his valuable pitching hand down. The baseball crashed against his bare pitching thumb and dribbled over toward second base, from where Darrel Chaney threw out Blanks.

"I reached down toward my knee with both hands . . . I think . . . I don't really remember much after that," Gullett said. Gullett flattened out on his stomach on the AstroTurf and yelled, "My thumb, my thumb." The baseball thudded so hard against the outer part of the thumb that it left stitch-marks the length of it." It was fractured.

The next day, Joe Morgan was sitting in his orange folding director's chair in a corner of the clubhouse when Gullett walked past, his thumb protruding in a cast, a sling strung around his neck to keep it immobile.

Morgan tossed aside a newspaper and glanced across the room, shaking his head in sympathy. But Morgan was not about to cast aside the season and concede to the Dodgers. "What does Gullett's loss mean to us? It means we win by five games instead of ten. I'm not knocking pitching or Gullett's role, but he only pitches every fifth day. It's not as if we lost Pete Rose, Tony Perez, Johnny Bench or me."

As it turned out, Morgan wasn't even half right. Instead of winning by 10, the Reds sashayed in by 20. Still, Anderson and the Reds were more than pleased when on Aug. 18, Gullett returned and pitched five scoreless innings in St. Louis.

It is no secret Don Gullett is Sparky Anderson's "boy." Although he is but 24, Gullett already owns 80 major league victories. "The kid is my prize," says Sparky. "I ain't taught him nothing. In fact, he taught me. He taught me how to achieve success and remain the same person. You don't have to be a prima donna.

"I bring all our new young pitchers into my office and shut the door," Sparky added. "I tell them to observe Gullett. Do yourselves a favor. Be like him, watch him, and act like him. If you do, you'll never have any problems here, unless you can't pitch. Don Gullett has never asked for a single favor. He wants no special treatment."

Getting Gullett to talk about himself is a difficult task, at best. On the day a Cincinnati scout watched him at McKell High School near his Lynn, Ky., home, Gullett pitched a perfect seven-inning game. He retired 20 of the 21 batters via strikeout. The 21st man was a chicken-heart. He bunted. Gullett threw him out.

In one football game, running back Don Gullett scored 72 points -- by himself. He scored 11 touchdowns and kicked six extra points.

"My coach was mad at the other coach," Gullett explained. "We had a pre-season scrimmage with this same school, our rival, Wortland. They beat us, 20-7, although we ran only three different plays and I had been hurt and not practicing much. The two coaches had some words in the papers and the Wortland coach bragged about how they stopped Gullett in the scrimmage."

NATURAL TALENT -- Don Gullett, shown being interviewed in the Reds clubhouse in Fenway Park, was an athletic star even in high school. In one high school football game, he scored 72 points.

Gullett's coach turned him loose in that game. On the game's first play, Gully intercepted a pass and returned it for a touchdown. Then the points came in torrents as Gullett carried almost every play. The final score was Gullett 72, Wortland 6. Gullett missed five extra points. "Guess my legs got tired," he grinned. "Oh, yeah," he added. "I had three touchdowns called back."

Now, Gullett was standing on the Fenway Park pitching mound; there 35,205 fans tucked into the pretty little park, most of them hating Gullett's guts at the moment.

Gullett's opponent was retread Luis Tiant, rescued from the scrap heap by the Boston Red Sox. The fans adored and idolized the balding Cuban with an ever-present post-game cigar. As he trudged in from

MOUND SESSIONS--Luis Tiant plans strategy with manager Darrell Johnson and Carlton Fisk above; Don Gullett confers with catcher Johnny Bench and pitching coach Larry Shepard below.

the bullpen before the game, chants of "Looie, Looie, Looie" thundered around his ears.

Gullett was shaky the first two innings, but kept escaping trouble - - even when the first two Bostonians reached base in the second. Tiant was untouchable, retiring the first 10 Reds, thanks to excellent defensive plays by first baseman Cecil Cooper on George Foster's line drive in the second and second basement Denny Doyle's backhanded stab of Ken Griffey's ground ball in the third.

But, with one out in the fourth, Joe Morgan singled and the first World Series turmoil erupted. National League umpire Nick Colosi called a balk on Tiant, the first called on him in his 11 years as a major league pitcher. The usual hub-bub ensued between Colosi and Boston Manager Darrell

Johnson. As usual, umpire wins, manager loses.

"He made a trick move with his knee," Colosi explains. "He was all right with his hands, but he jiggled the knee."

It didn't matter. Tiant and his St. Vitus dance motion got out of the inning. It was still 0-0 in the seventh when George Foster led with a single. In the three-game National League Playoffs with the Pirates, the Reds stole 11 bases without getting caught. Now, Foster tried to swipe second and catcher Carlton Fisk gunned him down.

Dave Concepcion followed with a stinging low liner to left, certainly a base hit. But Merv Rettenmund's earlier warning about the shallow left field played by left fielder Carl Yastrzemski came to pass. Yaz swooped in and made a diving, rolling, somersaulting catch - - coming up and holding the ball aloft.

Ken Griffey followed with a double and the Red Sox walked Cesar Geronimo intentionally. Gullett zinged a soft liner between first and second, but Denny Doyle streaked over and speared it . . . three super defensive plays, a clue The Big Red Machine was not up against the Cleveland Indians or Milwaukee Brewers.

"I don't make that catch on Concepcion in any other park in baseball," Yaz admits. "I have different theories about playing left field here. I play in very shallow. Why play on the warning track when any ball hit over your head is off the wall?"

The Boston seventh inning turned into a Cincinnati faux pas. The Bosox sent all six of their runs across home plate, all due to a couple of bad decisions.

El Tiante, as Bostonians call Louis, was the leadoff hitter. With the American League's Designated Hitter rule, Tiant had batted only one time in the last three seasons. Gullett struck him out the first time and walked him the second time. But, oh that third time. Quickly, Gully slipped two fast balls past him.

"I was sure he would throw me another fast one," said Tiant. "I see nothing but smoke the first two times and I have not batted in six months." The fast ball never came. Gullett tried to slip a fork ball past him, Don's version of the changeup. A high changeup. El Tiante jerked it into left field for a hit. Why, Donald, why?

"I wanted to keep it down and strike him out, but I got it up and he hit it," Gullett said softly later.

Dwight Evans bunted and Gullett pounced on the baseball. It didn't appear he would have time to get the slew-footed Tiant at second, the bunt was too good.

"I can't second guess what happened next," said Gullett. "I was facing home plate. Johnny Bench was in front of me and could see second base. He yelled, 'go to second, go to second.' It was my job to go to second. I lost my balance and didn't make a good throw."

The baseball skipped in front of shortstop Dave Concepcion and Tiant was safe, Evans reaching first. "Oh yeah," insisted Bench. "We had time. Even with Don's bad throw, we still almost had Tiant."

Anderson wouldn't admit it, but he hinted that decision might not have been the one he would have made. "I never second guessed my pitchers before, and I won't now. Not in public, anyhow."

Denny Doyle was going to bunt, too, but fouled it, a most unfortunate foul for the Reds. Bosox Manager Darrell Johnson wiped off the bunt sign. After swinging and missing, Doyle, a lefty, punched a base hit to left and Tiant moved to third, loading the bases with no

DEBATABLE BALK -- Red Sox pitcher Luis Tiant questions the umpire about a balk called on him in World Series game one.

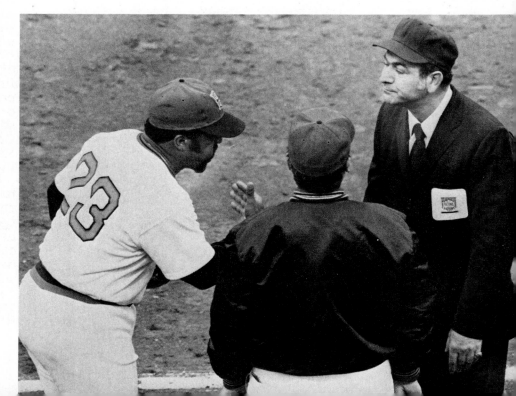

outs.

"I was pleased not to get the bunt sign after I popped the first try," Doyle said. "It's tough to get a guy like Tiant from second to third on a bunt. And, the Reds were giving me the hole between third and short. My idea was to punch it through on the ground. That's the way it worked."

Yaz was the man now and he blooped a single to right, scoring Tiant from third with the game's first run - - though Looie missed home and had to sneak back from the batting circle to touch it while shortstop Dave Concepcion was screaming for first baseman Tony Perez to throw the ball home.

That was the game's first run and ended Gullett's day. Clay Carroll pitched to Fisk and walked in the second run on a 3-and-2 pitch after he had him 1-and-2. Sparky immediately brought in lefty Will McEnaney to face lefty Fred Lynn. Mac struck him out, but Sparky - - going against his managerial whims of the regular season and against his promise to manage in the World Series just as he did in the regular season - - left McEnaney in to face righthanders Rico Petrocelli and Rick Burleson, instead of bringing in righthander Pedro Borbon, warming up in the bullpen.

"McEnaney is a sinker ball pitcher and I was hoping he could get Petrocelli to hit the ball on the ground for a double play," Sparky explained. Petrocelli singled for two runs and Burleson ripped his third hit of the day for another run. Cecil Cooper lobbed a deep sacrifice fly to the right field wall, scoring Petrocelli and the final score was on the board . . . Boston 6, Cincinnati 0.

The Red Sox had smashed Cincinnati's best pitcher and delighted their fans with spectacular defensive play and a five-hitter by their favorite Cuban, Luis Tiant.

After the game, his arm submerged up to his right elbow in an ice bucket and his lips curling around a long, thick Cuban cigar, El Tiante said it all in a few simple Spanish-inflected words. "When everything go right, everything go right. When everything go wrong, everything go wrong."

For nine innings, El Tiante strung zeroes across the scoreboard, plastered against the much-maligned, much-feared Green Monster of a left field wall, 315 feet from home plate and 37 feet tall. For three days, the Reds talked about almost nothing but, "The wall, the wall, oh my gosh, the wall."

Came the game and not once did the wall come into play. Neither team came close to projecting a baseball against the cement and tin Green Monster. Obviously, the Reds should have been talking more about El Tiante, a man from Havana with a curving mustache that makes him look to hitters like Pancho Villa must have looked to gringos.

For Boston fans, and many fans coast-to-coast, it was a heart-rendering game for Tiant. By the grace of Cuban Premier Fidel Castro, El Tiante's dad, Luis Tiant, Sr., sat in the stands and watched, sitting there with a special visa. Until late this season, dad had never seen son pitch in the major leagues.

The Reds, The Big Red Machine, were helpless this day, and down, one game to none in the 1975 World Series. Was this to be another letdown for Series-starved Cincinnati fans?

TAKING A DIVE -- Joe Morgan slips under the tag of Boston first baseman Cecil Cooper in World Series game one.

who will come out on top?

1975 RED SOX

REAR - L to R -- Rick Miller, Dick Drago, Luis Tiant, Rick Wise, Bill Lee, Jim Burton, Roger Moret, Dick Pole, Regie Cleveland.

2nd -- Equip. Mgr. Pete Cerrone, Trainer Charlie Moss, Doug Griffin, Bob Heise, Denny Doyle, Tim Blackwell, Cecil Cooper, Bob Montgomery, Dwight Evans, Juan Beniquez, Bernie Carbo, Diego Segui, Equip. Mgr. Vince Orlando.

1st -- Jim Rice, Carlton Fisk, Rico Petrocelli, Coach John Pesky, Coach Don Bryant, Manager Darrell Johnson, Coach Stan Williams, Coach Don Zimmer, Carl Yastrzemski, Rick Burleson, Fred Lynn.

Batboy Mike Naticchioni   Batboy Kenny Krall

FENWAY PARK WORKOUT

BIG WINNER -- Jack Billingham had more victories combined in 1973-74 than any pitcher in the Senior Circuit, winning 19 each season.

chapter five

A New England nor'easter arrived in a huff Sunday morning, turning Boston into an oyster-gray day fit for neither man nor whale. A steady drizzle pelted the Cincinnati Reds as they boarded the team bus, dampening their multi-colored leisure suits.

Sober faces were the order of the morning. Down 0-1 in the 1975 World Series to the Red Sox, the Reds faced the possibility of playing on a tacky field, slowing down their base-running capabilities. And, it was 54 degrees. The Reds, as do most ball players, prefer something like 84 degrees.

"This won't help us any," said outfielder Ken Griffey, glancing out the bus window.

"The Red Sox have to play in it, too," said George Foster.

"Except, the Red Sox are used to playing in this kind of weather," Griffey replied.

"But, we have the best thing going for us. We're the Cincinnati Reds," Foster said with finality.

The Boston Red Sox also had Bill Lee going for them, an eccentric lefthander who has solved every Boston problem but the school busing issue. And, Lord knows, he has tried to do that, too.

Jack Billingham started for the Reds and ran into immediate problems. Cecil Cooper lobbed a double to left on which Foster staggered around near the wall as if inebriated. But George doesn't drink anything stronger than a peanut butter milkshake. Cooper ended up on second base and Denny Doyle followed with a single off Billingham's glove.

Carl Yastrzemski also aimed one at Billingham. This time, Jack fielded it and immediately threw to second base for a force on Doyle. Cooper anchored himself at third until Billingham made his move toward second. Then, Cooper tried for home. Shortstop Dave Concepcion took the throw for the force on Doyle and zipped a throw home. Cooper was as dead as Julius Caesar, though he delayed his death via a rundown long enough for Yaz to sneak to second. From there, Yaz scored on Fred Lynn's single.

What might have been a big inning - - three of the first four Bostonians slammed hits - - turned into a one-run deal.

The Red Sox absent-mindedly lost another opportunity in the second when Dwight Evans was hit by a pitch and Rick Burleson singled. But, Evans strayed too far off second and catcher Johnny Bench caught him so far afield that Evans' only hope was to try for third. Shortstop Concepcion erased him easily.

Lee was well-nigh invincible through the ever-increasing raindrops. As El Tiante had done the day before, Lee retired the first ten Big Red Machinists. It ended when he walked Joe Morgan - - and that usually hurts an opposing pitcher to give Morgan a freebie. Ask any of the pitchers who walked him 132 times in 1975. Morgan advanced to third on Johnny Bench's single to right center and scored while Tony Perez was bouncing into a force play. Bench's unusual single to the opposite field was to be prophetic.

The Red Sox rid themselves of Billingham in the sixth with an unearned run when Yaz singled, took second on Concepcion's throwing error on Carlton Fisk, and scored when Rico Petrocelli slammed a 3-and-2 pitch into left field.

It was getting colder and wetter by the minute. Most of the some 500 newspaper guys abandoned their seats in the open pressbox and opted for a seat in the warmth of a heated press room on Fenway Park's roof, watching the game like most of the country, on TV. The rain finally delayed the game 27 minutes after the seventh inning with Boston up, 2-1.

When it resumed, the world was to see what made the Relentless Reds tick in 1975. Lee walked to the mound for the ninth with a 2-1 lead. It was not a pleasant thought, though. The first four Cincinnati hitters were to be John Bench, Tony Perez, George Foster and Dave Concepcion - - all right handed hitters powerful enough to knock a concrete block out of the Green Monster's belly.

On Lee's first pitch, Bench leaned out and flicked the

BATTLING THE ELEMENTS -- Lefthander Bill Lee of the Red Sox pitched in the cold and wet weather in game two of the Series. He lasted 6.1 innings, giving up 3 runs on 7 hits.

SHOULDER PROBLEMS - The omnipresent pain in John's left shoulder became worse when he attempted to pull the ball.

ball the opposite way again, to wide open right field, then thundered through the muck to second for a double. Lee's day was over and Dick Drago's short day began.

"The pitch to Bench was two inches outside and an inch above his knees," Lee was to say of the ill-fated double. "Today was the first time I've ever faced Bench and he hit a good breaking ball. If I had to do it over, I might change the pitch. The wind was blowing in from left. I should have thrown it up there and said, 'Here it is,' try to hit it over that big,' damn wall.''

Said Bench, "I thought the pitch was up, not down. That just shows you how I've been going. I even thought about bunting when I went up there. I think that wall, though, that Green Monster in left, makes me a better hitter. I know they are going to pitch me away and for once I used my intelligence instead of power and strength."

Drago, a fast-balling right hander, appeared to be out of the dilemma. Perez grounded to short as Bench took third. Foster, needing only a deep fly to left to score Bench with the tying run, fouled off four pitches, then popped to shallow left. The Red Sox were one out away from taking a 2-0 lead in the Series. They didn't get it.

"I made the last out of the first game," Dave Concepcion said. "I was 0-for-7 when I stepped in and I tell myself, No way I make last out today, even if I have to stick my head in front of the ball." After taking a ball, Concepcion bounced one past Drago over second. Denny Doyle stopped it, but couldn't throw as Bench literally stomped with both feet on home plate, tying it 2-2.

The Relentless Reds were

now going to show the nation's millions how they used their flying feet to swipe 169 bases in 205 attempts, an 82 per cent success ratio. Joe Morgan led the way with 68 thefts and only 10 caught stealings. Concepcion was next with 33 of 39.

Now, he was on first, the go ahead run and 90 feet of gooey turf between him and second base. Despite their gaudy, glistening statistics, the Reds were 0-for-2 in the Series. In the sixth, Fisk had pegged out Morgan. "No way does he get me on a fast track. Those were adverse conditions, we were running on a slow track," Morgan said. Ken Griffey, a man who legged out 39 infield hits in 1975 with searing speed, called the going "treacherous."

It didn't bother Concepcion. He glanced at third base coach Alex Grammas and picked up the steal sign - - but the muck almost caught him when he arrived. David stole it easily, but went sliding right past the bag in the mud. "If Doyle had hit me with a follow-up tag, I'm out and the inning is over," he said.

Instead, Ken Griffey rocketed a double to left center, chasing Concepcion home with the winning run. Griffey was searching for a fast ball and Drago offered it to him. "If I'm throwing good, with velocity, I don't fool around with anything but the fast ball," said Drago. "Most of the time this season it worked for me. Griffey hit a low and away pitch. When he hits a pitch like that, there's nothing I

can do."

The manipulating wasn't over, yet. Boston walked Cesar Geronimo on purpose to bring up Rawly Eastwick, who had arrived in the eighth and eliminated Dwight Evans on a called third strike with two on and two out. Cincinnati Manager Sparky Anderson's decision was one of these: Go for more runs with a pinch-hitter or let Eastwick bat and pitch the bottom of the ninth with a 3-2 lead.

Sparky chose to stay with Eastwick and he bounced into a forceplay, ending the inning. "I was sitting there wondering if Sparky would pinch-hit for me when he told me to grab a bat," Eastwick said. "I slammed on a batting helmet before he could change his mind. What a great feeling. He was

TO CATCH A THIEF-- Ken Griffey stole 16 bases in 23 attempts in '75.

THE LEADER -- Rawly Eastwick, receiving the ball from Sparky Anderson in the Series, led the Cincinnati staff in saves with 22.

telling me, 'The game is yours, go finish it up for us.' Sure, I wanted to stay in. I don't want anybody finishing up my job.''

Eastwick finished up brilliantly, retiring the Bosox 1-2-3 to gain the victory and level the Series at one-all heading back to Cincinnati. But, this game really belonged to Johnny Bench and his wrong-way double to start the ninth. And, what if he had bunted, as he said he thought about doing?

"If Bench, or any of my players, has a feeling, that's okay with me," said Anderson. "But I would have questioned Bench about it. No, I wouldn't have chewed him out if it wasn't successful, just questioned."

Bench made much over the fact, "I used my head in going to right field." But, the truth is, the aching shoulder makes it painful for Bench when he tries to pull the ball. Loaded with cortisone and pain most of the year, Bench still batted .283, hit 28 homers, drove in 110 runs and - - can you believe, this? - - stole 11 straight bases.

And, early in the season, Cincinnati fans booed his every popup, his every strikeout. It's always that way. For some unexplained reason, Cincinnati fans boo Johnny Bench. Fans on the road treat him as if he is the second coming of Babe Ruth.

The home treatment incensed Anderson, but Bench shrugs it off. "How a man could come to this club eight years ago and literally - - I mean literally - - put Cincinnati on the map, then get the treatment this man receives is beyond me," Sparky said. "Cincinnati was an also-ran in drawing fans until Bench came along. No man has the popularity in baseball John Bench has, especially on the road - - not

Bench and Anderson are in the midst of one of the Reds frequent pitching changes.

since Babe Ruth. I guarantee you, if you take a poll of every person in the United States, even if they've never seen a sporting event, and ask them who is America's No. 1 athlete, the winner is not Joe Namath. Bench wins the poll . . . easy," Sparky continued.

So why does Bench take the homefront abuse?

"You turn your TV on and you see John Bench," Anderson said. "He gets married this spring and 1,000

people show up, many of them celebrities. People are very jealous. There are people no longer awed by him. On the road, where people might see him only once or twice a year, it is a treat.''

Anderson devised a trick, a scheme, in Philadelphia for a quick exit from the clubhouse to the bus after a game. The Reds must wade through hundreds of fans to board. Sparky waits until he sees Bench leave the clubhouse and trails him.

"Works every time," says Sparky. "They see Bench first and mob him. Nobody bothers me and I walk right to the bus. Once in a while I forget and go out first. They ask me for autographs and I say, 'Okay, I'll sign 'em, but you're gonna miss Bench because he's on his way out.' That works every time, too. They leave me and crowd around the door."

Whenever a Benchian discussion comes up, Anderson invariably hears m-o-n-e-y . . . and the fact John makes too much of it, much more than his $175,000 salary. "People are always saying I protect Bench. He's my little bo-bo, they say. That's not so. Listen, no guy gets where he is as fast as Bench got there and didn't earn it."

Bench hears the grumbles, too, but is equipped with replies. "Jimmy Connors plays two tennis matches and makes $850,000. Muhammad Ali fights one bout and is paid $5 million. I play 190 games, counting exhibitions, and I'm overpaid," Bench answers. "A guy works 17 years preparing himself for a baseball career and the average player might last five years in the majors, if he's lucky. After that, he might be toting a lunch bucket. I don't believe I'm overpaid and I don't believe any ball player is overpaid."

After the home plate collision with Matthews on April 22, Bench's average dipped from .304 to .256 on a 7-for-48 slide. And the fans booed on. "I've been taking two pain pills a day and the shoulder has been hurting so much I can't sleep on my left side, the one I usually sleep on. Just doing this hurts," he said, stretching his left arm across his chest." That's the way it was for him all season.

The man is only 27 years old, but wise far beyond his years and a multi-personality. For a man 27, Johnny Lee Bench has been asked to do many things. And, for the most part, he not only did them, he did them with valor - - on and off baseball's playgrounds. But, when asked to write his own epitaph, Bench was stunned. For several seconds, he stared at his massive hands - - one of which can hold seven baseballs at once.

"I've never thought about dying," he said. "I guess I'd like to be known for not only who I was, but what I was. I'm sure I'll die and never be fully understood." That was a startling revelation to a listener who always believed Bench bared his heart right down to the aorta for sportdom's sometimes cruel public.

"I'm not understood in a lot of things," he said. "I don't talk a lot about my private feelings. I always carry them within myself. I've always been that way. It's hard on people around me. Vickie (his recent bride) doesn't understand this at all. I have to learn to change, but I don't know if I can."

Bench says this, and yet, it is contrary to outward appearances. As a humanitarian, no athlete does more than Bench. No athlete makes more free public appearances. "That's my background, my upbringing," he said. "I'm only 27, but I'm secure. I always associated and played with older kids, even when I was in Little League. I gained growing-up experience quicker than most kids and matured quick because of it. Most

HELPING HAND --"As a humanitarian, no athlete does more than Bench. No athlete makes more free public appearances."

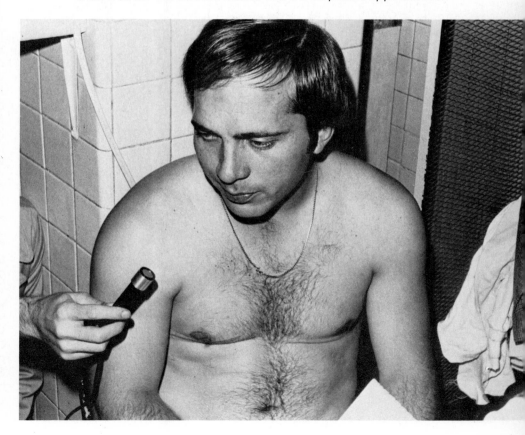

people my age, and a lot older, are insecure. This feeling of insecurity makes them unhappy and afraid of other people's feelings toward them. They live in their own little world and will not give of themselves.''

Bench says he has not thought about dying, but in December, 1972, those thoughts surely crossed his mind when a tumor was discovered in his chest. Though it was benign, the ugly scar of the operation still winds around his chest, a hideous red snake of a reminder.

''That experience made me my own man,'' Bench said. ''I conquered it and I came back. Because of that, I am no longer a man in a hurry. Nothing is the 'End of the World' type thing to me any more. It really took the sharp edge off me . . . made me easy-going. I no longer have the killer instinct. Now, it takes something very

BENCH entertains Sparky Anderson [left] and Alex Grammas with a golfing story before a home game.

dramatic to key me up.''

The humanitarian side of Bench shows up when he meets a kid like Philip Buckingham, a 4-year-old he met last year in Dayton, Ohio. Philip died of leukemia the day spring training opened this season, but Bench made his last days happy with frequent personal visits. Then, there was the illness of former major league pitcher Jim McGlothlin, an ex-Red. Bench put together a benefit show that netted close to $12,000 toward McGlothlin's hospital bills. After leaving baseball, McGlothlin dropped his insurance.

At the show, Bench unleashed another talent. He sang, a chilling rendition of Cat's in the Cradle. It was done so well, Bench's professional singing buddy, Bobby Goldsboro, would have been proud to say he sang it.

''I haven't thought much

about what I'd do when I get out of baseball,'' Bench says. ''I never had responsibilities. I was just out there playing baseball, traveling and having fun. Now that I'm married, I've been thinking about new avenues and the entertainment world intrigues me - - acting and singing.''

Before they retire Bench's uniform number ''5,'' maybe as the best all-around catcher in baseball history, John probably will scribble a thousand records into the Encyclopedia of Baseball. And yet, Bench remains the recipient of home town boos - - like the jerks who stand under a building and yell at a man perched on the 14th floor, ''C'mon, jump, will ya?''

''It's true,'' Bench realizes. ''I'm appreciated more on the road than at home. And, it's been tough, especially on my mom and dad . . . and now Vickie. I don't know what people expect. I drove in 129 runs in 1974 and I hear a smattering of boos on opening day before we've played a game. What do people expect?

''I try to avoid the booing controversy because if I fight back people say I think I'm too good to be booed,'' Bench says. ''Sure, it hurts. But I avoid talking about it. When we win, it's not so bad, I guess.''

Bench acknowledges that perhaps the booing is a backhanded compliment. People recognize his raw talent and expect something big every time he swings a bat or cocks his arm. ''Well, I expect a lot of myself, too,'' he says. ''I'm a tough critic on myself. But, I'll tell you - - give me the statistics I had in 1974 and I wouldn't even play a game in 1975 - - just chalk them up.'' In 1974, Bench drove in 129 runs, scored 108, hit 33 homers and

batted .280. ''Probably my best year - - and they booed,'' he grinned.

''Nobody likes to be booed,'' says Anderson. ''That's why I feel so sorry for John. I'm no different, I don't like it either. But I can put it in its right place. I don't think people are booing me personally. They are taking out their own frustrations. I guarantee, if we win 10 in a row and then lose the 11th game, they'd

unload on me, boo me when I walked out of the dugout. Around here, they don't want you just to win. They want you to annihilate the other team. The more you annihilate the other guys, the more the people show up.''

And that's why, after years of frustration, Cincinnati fans are ready to explode over a World Series championship.

THE CRASH-- The photo series which appears on the following three pages shows the home plate crash that caused Johnny Bench shoulder problems most of the '75 season. The collision took place on April 22 at Riverfront when San Francisco Giant outfielder Gary Matthews was ruled safe on the play.

chapter six

All season long, Ed Armbrister stood around batting cages making promises. "I'm the key," he would say. "When it all comes down to the end I'll be the big man."

His teammates laughed and hit each other in the ribs with elbows. Of all the Cincinnati Reds, Ed Armbrister, of the Grand Bahamas, is the closest thing to being a non-entity. During the season, Armbrister appeared only 59 times as a reserve outfielder, batting 65 times for an .185 average. He drove in two runs, hit one double and blew one game in San Diego by dropping a fly ball.

In the final game of the National League Playoffs, Armbrister came through with his promise, the promise his buddies took as a joke. It was nothing like a grand slam home run, or even a broken bat single. It

was a fly ball, a sacrifice fly that scored Ken Griffey with the run that broke a 3-3 tie in the top of the ninth and provided the pennant-clinching run in a 5-3 Cincinnati victory.

As the champagne ran in small streams across the clubhouse floor, Armbrister kept saying, "I told 'em. They wouldn't listen, but I told 'em I'd be a big man at the end."

But, not as big as he would become in Game Three of the 1975 World Series.

Home runs were the order of the evening in Game Three, not in cramped Fenway Park, but in spacious Riverfront stadium. First, it was Carlton Fisk, leading off the Boston second. Then, it was Johnny Bench, driving one over the left field wall in the Cincinnati fourth after Tony Perez walked and stole second--one of three Cincinnati thefts as the Big

Red Machine finally found its wheels.

The Red Sox tied it in the fifth on two walks, a wild pitch by relief pitcher Pat Darcy--in for starter Gary Nolan--and a sacrifice fly.

Cincinnati's offensive muscle flexed in the fifth when Dave Concepcion and Cesar Geronimo unleashed back-to-back homers off starter Rick Wise. Pete Rose tripled and scored on Morgan's sacrifice fly, providing the Reds with a 5-2 lead and the 55,392 fans much to yell about.

Pinch-hitter Bernie Carbo, once a Cincinnati Red, lobbed Darcy's first pitch of the seventh inning over the left field barrier, but the Reds were in charge, 5-3, going into the ninth. Will McEnaney struckout Fred Lynn, a left hander. Anderson again went against his managerial philosophy. Instead of immediately bringing in right hander Rawly Eastwick to face a bevy of right handed hitters, he let McEnaney pitch to Rico Petrocelli.

Rico shoved a single to center. Now, Sparky brought in Eastwick and Dwight Evans hit a 331-foot homer over the 330-sign in the left field corner, tying the game, 5-5, and keeping millions of TV watchers from slipping between the covers of their beds for a good night's sleep.

Cincinnati's Cesar Geronimo opened the Reds' tenth with a single. Ed Armbrister and American League umpire Larry Barnett were about to become national celebrities--something neither had done in their baseball careers. With Geronimo on first, Armbrister was sent up to bat for Eastwick and his instructions were simple: "Bunt Geronimo to second." Simplicity ended there.

Armbrister's bunt hit the ground and bounced into the air, about six feet in front of the plate. Armbrister took two steps forward and Fisk climbed over him after the baseball, a bumping incident ensuing. Fisk grabbed the ball, poised correctly, cocked his arm nicely, and fired the ball toward second.

It sailed over Rick Burleson's head and Geronimo motored to third and Armbrister to second.

Eventually, Geronimo scored the game-winning run on Joe Morgan's one-out, bases-loaded, line drive single over drawn-in center fielder Fred Lynn . . . the game was over, but the controversy wasn't. As Geronimo tapped home, Fisk turned and hurled his mask against the screen, leaving it there.

There were more dirty words polluting the Boston clubhouse air than one hears in an XXX-rated porno flick.

WAS IT INTERFERENCE? This sequence of photos show the controversial play during the 10th inning of World Series Game No. 3 in Cincinnati between Boston's Carlton Fisk and Cincinnati's Ed Armbrister at home plate. Home plate umpire Larry Barnett's decision that Armbrister did not interfere with Fisk caused a national controversy and even led to a death threat against Barnett. Pictures were taken from NBC-TV.

EYE OF THE STORM --
After Carlton Fisk and Ed Armbrister collided at home plate in the famed ''no interference'' bunt play, the Boston catcher threw wildly to second base. Cesar Geronimo (on right) watches Fisk's throw roll into centerfield; Geronimo came home to win the game later in the inning (below).

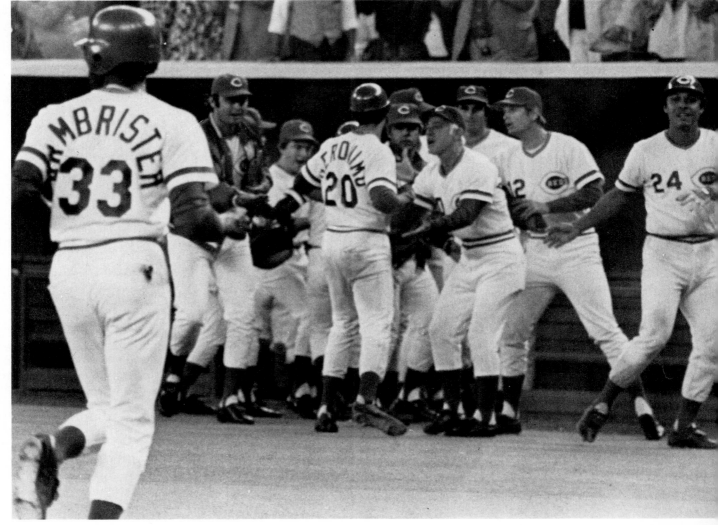

To a man, the Red Sox felt they were publicly mugged by umpire Barnett.

"Umpires 2, Red Sox 1," screamed Boston shortstop Rick Burleson. Actually, it was Cincinnati 2, Red Sox 1 after three games.

Fisk spat on the clubhouse carpet and spiraled a $2 World Series program from his dressing bench to across the room, pages fluttering. "It's a joke to lose a World Series game that way," Fisk finally fumed after remaining silent a few moments, words eventually gushing from within in torrents. "Armbrister interfered with me. I don't know the rule, but I know a man can't run into me when I am trying to field the ball," Fisk added.

Fisk contradicted himself with that statement later when he explained how the play unfolded. "Armbrister bunted the ball and it went straight up," Fisk said. "Then, he stood there in front of the plate. I had to climb over him, go up for a rebound, to get the damn baseball." In other words, Carlton was now saying he went over Armbrister and Armbrister did not run into him?

"Hell, no," Fisk yelled. "I'm an infielder and I have a right to go after a ground ball. It's interference when a baserunner gets in the way of an infielder. He was out of the batter's box...Hell, I probably tagged him when I pushed him out of my way, but the damn umpire blew that one, too." (TV replay showed Fisk wrong on that one, too. He did not tag Armbrister, though he easily could have if he tried)

"The collision caused me to throw high to second, but the ball probably should have been caught anyway," Fisk yelled on. "It's an easy double play. Instead, the umpire blows it and we lose

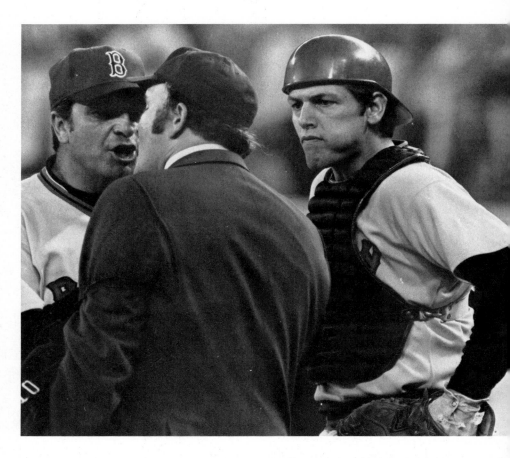

THE GREAT DEBATE--"To a man, the Red Sox felt they were publicly mugged by umpire Barnett."

a World Series game."

Barnett, a chubby-cheeked fellow from Prospect, Ohio, was working his first World Series. Barnett, who resembled singer Wayne Newton, patiently explained his call. "The batter was going to first. The catcher was going after the ball. There was no intentional contact, it can't be interference. The rules cover it."

Barnett explained that to Fisk and Boston Manager Darrell Johnson. The Boston manager was not satisfied, so Barnett asked him to

check with first base umpire Dick Stello, a National Leaguer. Stello's interpretation was the same, "No malice aforethought, no interference."

"The umpire's interpretation was different than mine," said Johnson. "In my opinion, the man (Fisk) was interferred with. The instant replay bears it out (no it didn't, Darrell). The umpire's statement about intention is irrelevant. It was a judgment call and he would not change his judgment."

Once again, the much-ignored Armbrister was the center of the press's attention as he stood in the Cincinnati clubhouse peeling off uniform number 33.

"I hesitated after bunting to watch," Armbrister admitted. "Yes, I was out of the box, about two steps in front of the plate. Fisk was coming from behind to make the play. I watched for a split second, then he hit me. When he hit me, I don't know if he was going for the ball or already had it. I know if I didn't hesitate, he would have had a better chance at the ball and the collision knocked me off balance. Why did I hesitate? Well, I could see where the ball was (in front of Armbrister) and I knew Fisk would be coming. If I had waited, then run into him, it would be interference. But, he ran into me."

After villifying Barnett, the Red Sox tore into the method used for selecting World Series umpires—which is not a selection system. Before last year, a rating system was used and the highest-rated men received the umpiring assignments. The umpires fought for, and succeeded, in getting it changed so that it is now a rotation system, all umpires taking turns. None of the six men working the 1975 World Series ever worked one before.

"Rotation my ass," screamed Carl Yastrzemski. "This is supposed to be baseball's finest hour. If they want rotation, let 'em rotate the teams, too. Every 12 years, your team plays in the Series. Next year, let San Diego and Milwaukee play in it."

Umpire Larry Barnett was excited about working his

first World Series six days before as he waited for his luggage to roll off the conveyor in the Boston Logan airport. Now, it turned into a nightmare. A gambler, admitting he lost considerable cash on Game Three, threatened Barnett's life. Baseball commissioner Bowie Kuhn took the threat seriously enough to provide the young umpire with body guards and tight security the rest of the Series. There were no incidents, though Barnett was booed lustily every time he appeared in Fenway park and his name was announced.

After the Series ended, Barnett and umpire Satch Davidson were on a flight from Boston to Columbus, Ohio. Dayton sports editor Si Burick spotted Barnett and engaged him in conversation. Barnett was prepared for a long winter of

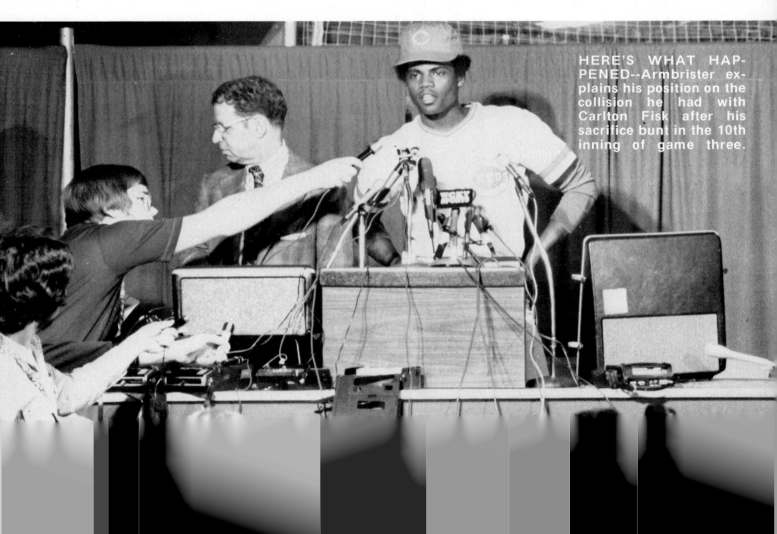

HERE'S WHAT HAPPENED--Armbrister explains his position on the collision he had with Carlton Fisk after his sacrifice bunt in the 10th inning of game three.

explanation. He pulled a Xeroxed copy of a rule from the umpire's casebook...and interpretation of rule 7:06(a):

"...when a catcher and batter/runner going to first base have contact, when the catcher is fielding the ball, there is generally no violation and nothing should be called."

It is clearly stated. But, because the man made his call, caring not who won or lost, his life and that of his family was threatened. It makes one wonder sometimes if it is all worth it.

The Armbrister-Fisk controversy took away from a heart-tugging story in Game Three. Cincinnati's starting pitcher was Gary Nolan, a guy who thought his baseball career might be over last year, but refused to admit it. Out of baseball two years, Nolan underwent an operation that corrected shoulder problems and came back to win 15 games. In 211 innings, Nolan walked only 29 hitters and carried a 3.16 earned run average.

On nights he didn't pitch, Nolan was an extrovert, one of the funniest among many humorous Cincinnati Reds. On nights after he pitches, the emotionally-drained Nolan talks in a subdued whisper - - as if awed by what he had done. Perhaps he was . . . and perhaps he should be.

"What Gary Nolan did is one of the most amazing and unbelievable performances in the history of baseball," said pitching coach Larry Shepard. "After being away from the game so long, it is an utterly fantastic story. Every time he went out and did well, he proved to himself he could do it. There had to be some doubts in his mind."

Nolan pitched very little since the 1972 All-Star game because of shoulder pains, pains that were alleviated in May of 1974 by an iffy operation performed by Dodger team physician Dr. Frank Jobe.

"When you are away from something you love and hold dear and think you might not ever be able to do it any more, it puts some severe thoughts in your coconut," Nolan said one night after retiring the first 15 Pirates in a 6-1 victory. "This was to be a year that I would go out and work hard, get things together again. I had no goals on how many wins. I just wanted to start 30 to 35 games (he started 32), pitch well in most of 'em, and keep us in the games. I think I did that most of the time."

It was an unbelievable comeback for a 27-year-old guy who only a year ago left

ACCOMPLISHED GOALS: "I just wanted to start 30 to 35 games, pitch well in most of 'em, and keep us in the game," Gary Nolan said. "I think I did that most of the time."

spring training thinking he had worn his last baseball uniform. It was two months before his operation and Nolan just couldn't hack it in spring training. As an airplane whisked him from Tampa, Florida to his Oroville, Calif., home, Nolan stared out a window at the billowy clouds and asked himself: "Will I ever be back to pitch? What's going to happen to me? All I've known is baseball."

"I just prayed after the operation that I'd be able to be back on the scene, maybe appear in 10, 15, 18 games, maybe in relief. I just wanted to be available to Manager Sparky Anderson." A year later, the spring of 1975, Nolan was super-sensational. "I was convinced I'd be able to take the ball and perform again. Not once have I had pain," he said. "I've been comfortable all along and I've been told I won't have any pain. It was a miracle from God."

So there was Nolan, on October 14, 1975, standing on the mound in front of 55,392 fans, pitching in a World Series game. He was good, very good. In four innings, he gave up one run (Fisk's homer) and three hits - - as usual, keeping the Reds "in the game," until Armbrister and Fisk could decide it in the tenth, sending the Reds into Game Four with a 2 games to 1 lead.

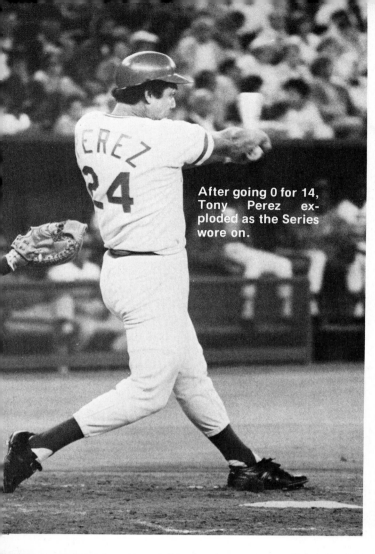

After going 0 for 14, Tony Perez exploded as the Series wore on.

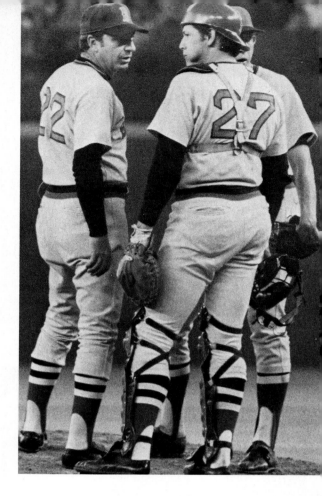

STRATEGY-- With the Reds hitters finding their stride, Boston Manager Darrell Johnson had to be on his toes at all times. Above, he consults with Carl Fisk and his pitcher, and below he observes closely from bench.

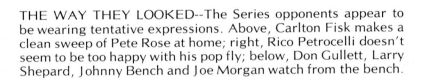

THE WAY THEY LOOKED--The Series opponents appear to be wearing tentative expressions. Above, Carlton Fisk makes a clean sweep of Pete Rose at home; right, Rico Petrocelli doesn't seem to be too happy with his pop fly; below, Don Gullett, Larry Shepard, Johnny Bench and Joe Morgan watch from the bench.

SIDELINE ACTION -- Bob Howsam and Commissioner Bowie Kuhn confer (above); the reporters gather around the batting cage before the game (below).

chapter seven

In contrast to the dismal weather in Boston, the sun baked down on the AstroTurf in Riverfront stadium, a remarkable Indian summer day in Southwestern Ohio as the Cincinnati Reds took batting practice in the twilight before Game Four of the World Series, leading 2 games to 1.

As usual, swarms of newspapermen were surrounding Pete Rose, Joe Morgan, Johnny Bench . . . even rookie Rawly Eastwick.

"We're not going back to Boston," Rose told writers as they furiously scribbled with Bics into their spiral notebooks. "We'll wrap it up right here, win the next two."

"We're in a big league ball park now," said Morgan. "We're still not playing baseball like we should, though. We blew a 5-1 lead before we won last night (Game Three, 6-5) and we just don't blow leads like that. But, we're the best, we'll win the next two." Again, reporters wrote it all down.

Manager Sparky Anderson told the media, "We're the best in baseball over the course of a season, but there are times we play so bad we should stay home."

Morgan, though, never lets it stop at a sentence or two. "We can play better, a lot better . . . and we'll do it. I'm not overly pleased with the way we played the first three games, but I'm not disappointed. Let's face it, there were some adjustments that had to be made in our minds," Morgan added. "We thought too much about The Wall in Boston, so we had to adjust to the park.

"Our pitchers were afraid to move the ball around for fear of making a mistake that would end up over the wall. I was a bit embarrassed because we have not put any pressure on Boston. We have not been ourselves. We're not taking the initiative, not making things happen like we did all season. But, we WILL win the World Series."

Eastwick, the winning pitcher in both Cincinnati games, may be only a rookie, but he has the Cincinnati inbred confidence. "I have a feeling we won't need to pack our suitcases to go back to Boston. We'll win it here," he said.

While the writers engulfed the super-stars, Cincinnati rookie infielder Doug Flynn stood off by himself, drinking it all in, until one writer approached him.

"All this is exciting, you know?" Flynn said to the writer. "The last two games, I've really been excited watching from the dugout. Since the playoffs and World Series, you're the first writer to talk to me or ask me a question,'' Flynn grinned. ''And I appreciate it. It's pretty tough on guys like me, Darrel Chaney and Bill Plummer. We don't blame the writers, we understand being ignored because we know they want to talk to the big guys,'' he said. ''Who wants to talk to guys who sit in the dugout screaming their lungs out?''

The 24-year-old rookie batted 128 times in 88 games during the season after the Reds signed him in a tryout camp. Flynn's college buddies at the University of Kentucky persuaded Doug to attend the camp because he was a sensational pickup softball player. Flynn was a scholarship basketball player at Kentucky, but lost out on grades.

When he made the Reds this spring, he was so awed with the travel he carried a camera on trips, snapping pictures of the Empire State Building, the Liberty Bell, the Hollywood Bowl, the Gateway Arch, the Golden Triangle and strangers on the street. Once on the team bus, Rose patted him on the back and said, ''Hang in there, kid. We're gonna win

THE ROOK-- 24 year old rookie Doug Flynn received a comforting word from Pete Rose during the regular season -- ''Hang in there, kid,'' Rose said. ''We're gonna win ya $25,000.''

ya $25,000."

And once Flynn fell victim to an old gag when Rose asked him if he knew where to find the key to the batter's box. Flynn didn't fully hear the question, so when he hesitated answering, the Reds roared with laughter, thinking Flynn believed there might be a "key to the batter's box."

The wide-eyed kid from Lexington, Kentucky so enjoyed the post-game confusion in the clubhouse after Game Two in Boston, he turned his chair around to face the center of the room and watched the panorama of writers and broadcast media tramping over one another.

"Know what I'm doing in the dugout?" Flynn asked. "I'm using one of those scorecards they pass out to the press and I'm keeping score of the games in the dugout."

Meanwhile, 57 writers were still gathered around Morgan and Joe continued his monologue. The Reds were 64-17 in Riverfront stadium in 1975 and somebody wanted to know if Morgan thought Boston would be worried about

Cincinnati's invincibility at home. "I hope so," he said. "If they let it bother them, that's fine with us. This is a major league ball park," he continued. "No freak walls to hold doubles to singles, no way to play shallow in the outfield and make catches on balls that should be hits. No, sir . . . no freak elements here."

Then, the game began, and the only freak element in Riverfront was Boston pitcher Luis Tiant. El Tiante admits to 34 years of life, but fellow Cuban Tony Perez of the Reds says with a grin, "When I was four, Tiant was just starting to play professional baseball. Now he is 34 and I am 33."

The Reds were one hit away from ridding themselves of Loo-ie in the first inning, but overexuberance did them in. Pete Rose opened the Cincinnati first with a single to center. Ken Griffey plastered one off the left centerfield wall and Rose scored. But Griffey tried to make his flying feet carry him to a triple and he was wiped away at third, centerfielder Fred Lynn to shortstop Rick Burleson to third baseman Rico Petrocelli.

Joe Morgan walked and took second on Perez's ground ball. Johnny Bench doubled to center, scoring Morgan - - a hit that also would have scored Griffey and made it 3-0 with one out. Tiant probably would have been lifted. Instead, it was 2-0 and Tiant remained on the mound to retire George Foster.

That's the way it stayed until the fourth when Boston emasculated Fred Norman with five runs and six hits, highlighted by a two-run triple by Dwight Evans, a run-scoring double by Burleson and a run-scoring single by Tiant off relief

OUT AT THIRD-- "Ken Griffey plastered one off the left centerfield wall and Rose scored. But Griffey tried to make his flying feet carry him to a triple and he was wiped away at third..."

pitcher Pedro Borbon.

Tiant's only other major difficulty arrived in the bottom of the fourth when the Reds scored twice after Tiant retired Perez and Bench to start the inning. But, Foster singled, Dave Concepcion doubled and Cesar Geronimo's opposite field triple into the left field corner sliced Tiant's advantage to 5-4.

Manager Sparky Anderson dispatched pinch-hitter Terry Crowley to home plate, a man who reached base eight straight times during one stretch of the season with six hits and two walks as a pinch-hitter. Tiant fanned him.

Neither team offered much in the way of offense until the Reds came to bat in the bottom of the ninth. When Geronimo opened the inning with a 2-and-2 line drive single to right, there wasn't a fan among the 55,667 who didn't think The Relentless Reds were about to do it again.

In a strange twist, Anderson again sent Armbrister up to bunt, setting up another possible controversy. Nothing happened this time. Armbrister's bunt was much harder, a bunt that forced Tiant to make the play and Geronimo, the tying run, stormed into second. Tiant

really tempted the gods by walking Rose, the winning run, and bringing up Ken Griffey, Cincinnati's best clutch hitter in the Series up to this time.

El Tiante offered Griffey five fast balls and the count stretched out to 3-and-2. The sixth pitch was a high, outside fast ball, the same type pitch Griffey

slaughtered off Dick Drago in Game Two to score Dave Concepcion with the winning run. Griffey murdered this one, too.

"He hit it a ton, crushed it," said Boston catcher Carlton Fisk. "The ball game's over," Fisk thought to himself.

Center fielder Fred Lynn turned and fled for the

KIND WORDS FROM THE SKIPPER-- Manager Sparky Anderson on George Foster: "He is the strongest guy on this club. When he hits the ball, it jumps off his bat."

CATCHING UP IN GAME FOUR--
"Foster singled, Dave Concepcion
doubled and Cesar Geronimo's
opposite field triple into the left field
corner (shown in photo sequence)
sliced Tiant's advantage to 5-4."

centerfield wall, 404 feet away. "I said to myself, 'Self, you gotta get goin' right now,'" Lynn said. "Usually when the ball is halfway to you, you can tell if you have a shot at it. I felt I had a chance."

Just before flesh meshed with wooden fence, Lynn flung his glove over his right shoulder and stabbed the spiraling baseball, a radiantly beauteous catch. "Can I rate its difficulty? I rated the catch pretty difficult when I was out there," Lynn said. "I didn't know if I could get my arm up."

Even with the catch, the Reds were still alive. Joe Morgan was the hitter with two outs. Tiant threw ball one, then for some reason, of his own volition, Geronimo broke for third on the second pitch. Morgan popped to the first baseman, ending the game.

"I didn't know Geronimo would be running," said Morgan. "When I don't know a guy is stealing and he breaks for a base, it breaks my concentration. The pitch was a low fast ball over the middle of the plate, a pitch I can pull. But, I lost my concentration and missed it."

When Lynn made his game-saving catch, Rick Miller was in left field. "I'm normally a center fielder," Miller said. "So, I know what that ball looked like to Freddie. I wanted to shout, 'Get back, get back; God, Freddie, get back.' But the crowd was yelling so loud, I could have had a megaphone and he wouldn't have heard me."

Griffey's game-winning double in Game Two hurt him in Game Four.

"I cheated over a little on him toward left center to start with because he beat us Sunday with a ball to left center," said Lynn. "I was nervous, too. I have to admit it. I kept thinking what would happen if those guys beat us again in the last inning the way they had in the last two games. For the first time I can remember, I was a little nervous."

Second baseman Denny Doyle wasn't nervous, or worried. "I've seen Freddie make so many great plays, I expect him to catch everything hit out there until I see it hit the ground."

Lynn's catch literally sent the Reds packing. Even though there was one more game scheduled in Cincinnati, the Reds could go home and pack their suitcases. They couldn't wrap it up in Cincinnati now . . . at least one game was assured in Boston. The Series was tied, 2-2.

BACK TO BOSTON-- The Red Sox were a happy group after they had won game 4. It meant that the two clubs had to go back to Boston to wrap up the Series.

RED HOT IN THE FIELD--One of the reasons the Big Red Machine was able to win 108 regular season games was their superb fielding. Cincinnati made only 102 errors, the least of any National League club.

THE FANNER-- Fred Norman [right] led the Reds pitching staff with 119 strikeouts in '75.

CONTACT MAN -- Joe Morgan seldom fails to make contact at the plate. In 1975, he struck out 52 times in 498 at bats.

HARD HITTERS--Dwight Evans (left) and Rico Petrocelli produced a total of 15 hits in the Series.

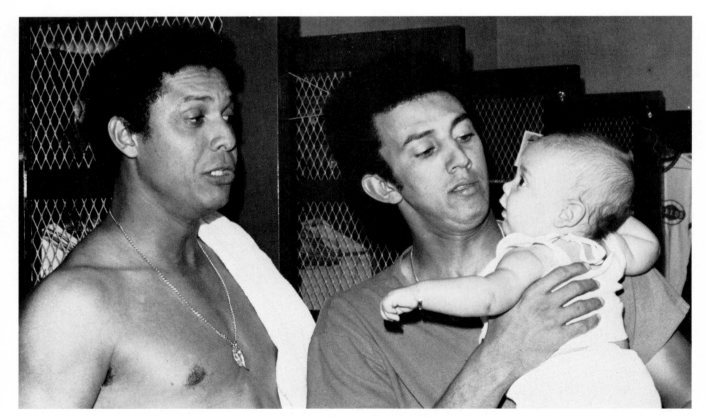

DAVEY MEET DOGGIE--Dave Concepcion introduces his son Davey to ''Doggie'' Perez.

chapter eight

Atanasio Rigal Perez, a smile his constant companion, was pulling on Cincinnati uniform number 24 before Game Five, alone with his thoughts. Certainly, Tony was wondering when he would get a hit. In the first four games, Perez was 0-for-14 with six strikeouts...this from a man who batted .314 after the All-Star break and hit .398 in August.

Manager Sparky Anderson walked by and interrupted Perez's thoughts with a well-aimed needle. "Just think, Tony," Sparky said. "If you can go the entire Series without a hit, your kids can tell their kids that grandpa holds the all-time World Series record for most at bats with no hits."

As always, Perez smiled. Perez would smile at a mugger in Central Park who took his last $100,000.

Tony Perez smiled all winter when the Cincinnati Reds tried to trade him for a third baseman and/or a pitcher. Perez signed with the Reds in 1960 and made the big club in 1964. As a ten-year man, Tony could veto any deal the Reds made. But, in typical fashion last winter, Perez said, "I know, if they get right offer, I gone. If I have to go, I make no trouble. I go."

The Reds couldn't come up with the right deal, so when the season opened, there was Perez at his old first base home. It probably was the best deal the Reds never made. After a miserable start during which Perez hovered near .200 for two months, Tony finished the season with a .282 average, 20 homers and 109 RBI. On September 2 against San Diego's Jerry Johnson, Perez became Cincinnati's all-time run producer with his 1,010th career RBI.

Now, he was sitting in front of his dressing stall wondering if he would erase Dal Maxvill from the World Series record book, 0-for-22, the height of futility.

"I never get down," Perez said. "My wife, Pituka, take me downtown before today's game to do some shopping for a change of scenery. People clap me on back and tell me to hang in there. And I get telegrams from people telling me to keep trying.

"Pituka make me drive different ways to the ball park and do different things before a game. She lock me in my room and make me watch television and sleep."

As Tony and Pituka breezed down Columbia parkway in their Oldsmobile Toronado, Perez broke a moment's silence with, "I hope I bat fifth or sixth tonight. There are no hits for me in the fourth spot."

To Tony's delight, when he gazed at the lineup card hanging in the dugout, Sparky had penned Perez into the fifth spot, moving Johnny Bench from fifth to fourth.

Cincinnati's Don Gullett was facing Boston's Reggie Cleveland when the game began and the largest crowd in Cincinnati's 107-year history, 56,393, was hardly seated when the Red Sox struck for a run. Denny Doyle tripled into the right field corner and scored on Carl Yastrzemski's deep fly to right.

The Reds tried to get something started in the bottom of the first when Pete Rose opened with a single. After Ken Griffey struck out, Joe Morgan singled Rose to third, then stole second. Johnny Bench lofted a medium-deep fly ball to left and Rose tired to score after the catch. Juan Beniquez pegged him out.

Perez led off the Cincinnati second and struckout on three pitches...0 for 15 with seven strikeouts. Tony didn't throw his bat, didn't kick his batting helmet, didn't yell at the bat boy. He shrugged and smiled.

Boston still clung to that 1-0 lead in the fourth and Cleveland retired the first two Cincinnatians. With Perez next, the 1-0 lead seemed secure. But, Reggie learned a lesson...never hang a slider, even to a guy struggling. Perez hung the slider over the left centerfield wall where 375 is painted and the fans went berserk.

"Well, you ruined your chance for immortality with that homer," Anderson said as Tony arrived in the raucous dugout. "No, no, skeeper. I no even want to know who holds that record," Perez grinned.

The Reds took charge the next inning, again with two outs. Gullett, as he did so often during the season, helped himself with a single,

SCORING PLAYS--"Denny Doyle tripled into the right field corner and scored on Carl Yastrzemski's deep fly to right." (above); Perez ruined his chances for immortality with his homer (below).

then toured the bases as Pete Rose doubled the opposite way into the left field corner, giving Cincinnati a 2-1 lead.

The sixth inning was the big one for Cincinnati, though after Cleveland walked Joe Morgan to start the inning, it looked as if the game would never end. Reggie threw over to first base 16 times to hold Morgan on--and if that isn't a record...well, most people never want to see if broken.

"I like to throw over there a lot," said Cleveland, a rotund fellow with a protruding stomach that drapes over his pants. "It's not just to keep the runner close, but it messes up the batter, too. He gets anxious, wants to swing."

Morgan did try to steal second once, but Bench fouled off the pitch. On a 2-and-2 pitch, second baseman Denny Doyle broke for the bag. But, there was a problem--Morgan wasn't running. Bench poked a base hit to right, the ball skipping through the infield right where Doyle would have been stationed had he not broken for the base.

"The ball came straight out of Bench's uniform," said Doyle. "I never saw it until it got even with the mound. I didn't move until Bench hit the ball, but I was playing close enough to make the play if I could only have seen the ball."

Instead, Morgan moved to third, giving the Reds runners on first and third with none out. And, Tony Perez was the hitter.

Perez, flushed with success, did it again. On a 1-and-2 pitch, Tony bashed the ball to the same spot, only deeper and more rewarding, a three-run concussion that gave the Reds a 5-1 lead. Perez had placed himself in the World Series record book all right,

KEEPING HIM CLOSE--"Reggie Cleveland threw over to first base 16 times to hold Morgan on."

on the positive instead of the negative side. He was only the 23rd man to hit two homers in a Series game and the first for the National league in 16 years.

That was the ball game, because the Red Sox could do nothing with Gullett's high-rise fast ball until the ninth inning. The Reds made it 6-1 in the eighth on two walks and a couple of fly balls.

After Doyle's first-inning triple, Gullett retired 16 straight. He walked Juan Beniquez, then sloughed off nine of the next ten, yielding a single to Dwight Evans in the eighth.

He didn't get through the ninth, though he retired the first two Bostonians. Carl Yastrzemski singled, Carlton Fisk singled and Fred Lynn doubled for a run.

Sparky Anderson made his move, signaling for Rawly Eastwick. Gullett quietly left to the standing plaudits of the 56,393. Eastwick did his work quickly, striking out Rico Petrocelli on three straight fast balls. The Reds were 6-2 winners, 3-2 leaders in the World Series, and one game away from winning their first World Series in 35 years.

After the game, a photographer asked Perez to kiss the bat that propeled the two homers, and Tony planted a smooch smack on the trademark.

"It's an R-43 model," Perez said. For those not familiar with the Louisville Slugger coding system, the R-43 was designed for George Herman (Babe) Ruth.

"No, no," Perez corrected. "Babe Ruth, he use MY model bat." On July 7, Perez had used that bat to slam a baseball into the left field red seats, Riverfront's upper deck. Only three baseballs have reached the deck, 35 feet above the ground, since

they opened Riverfront five seasons ago. On this day, a Steve Carlton slider on a 3-and-2 reached those seats. It was the second time Perez reached that plateau. The other perpetrator was Bob Bailey, then of Pittsburgh.

The day Perez hit his second one, a writer asked him if he remembered the first. "You kidding, man?"

Perez said. "When you hit 'em like that, you remember 'em. It was against New York's Jim McAndrew and it was with the bases loaded. Like this one, it was into the second row."

Perez winked at his interviewers that night and said, "I don't think Babe Ruth ever hit one that far, did he?" Then, after pausing

EXIT GULLETT--"Gullett quietly left to the standing plaudits of the 56,393..."

for effect, Perez added, "Righthanded."

Whenever Perez slips into a slump, as he did in the first four games of the Series, batting instructor Ted Kluszewski takes Perez by the hand and leads him under the stands, not for a paddling, but for a session in the batting cage. Klu brings out a batting tee, sits baseballs on it about waist high, and has Perez smash the stationary baseballs.

"When Tony goes into a slump, he pulls off the ball, doesn't keep his head in there," Klu said. "The tee helps him keep his head still. And, in batting practice, I make Tony concentrate on hitting the ball to right field--that makes him stay longer with the pitch. What happened tonight, those two homers, is something I knew would happen soon. His timing in snapping out of the slump was perfect, wouldn't you say?"

After the batting practice session, Perez walked over to Joe Morgan and said, "The pitcher is in trouble tonight. He is going to pay for my frustrations."

Reggie Cleveland paid. But, even if Perez had struckout four times and the Reds had lost, he would have greeted everybody after the game with that wide, toothy smile.

Tony Perez is 6-feet-2, weighs a little more than 200 pounds and is blessed with enough muscle tissue to clear a bar single-fistedly if he desired. And, isn't that hot Latin blood pumping through his body? It sure is, Cuban variety. But, Perez is walking proof that one can't generalize about a person's nationality dictating his temperament. There is more Cuban sugar flowing through his system than boiling Latin plasma.

In his 12 years with the Cincinnati Reds, his closest brush with a fight was a quick exchange of words with St. Louis pitcher Bob Gibson as he crossed the pitcher's mound. Other than that, Perez is a living billboard for the United Nations peace policy.

Once, Lee May took his position away from him. What did Perez do? He became bosom buddies with Lee May. Pete Rose took his position away from him once, too. Tony's reaction? Well, count Rose as one of Tony's closest friends.

For Perez, it all started in 1960 when he signed with the Havana Sugar Kings of the International League. The club was owned by Bobby Maduro, truly Havana's sugar king...along with

ON PEREZ: "There is more Cuban sugar flowing through his system than boiling Latin plasma."

THE ONE AND ONLY -- This sequence shows Tony Perez picking up his only stolen base of the Series.

Tony cradles one in.

being king of a lot of other Cuban businesses. The Reds signed a working agreement with Maduro until Fidel Castro claimed a little property, like the entire country.

"I was working in sugar factory in Camaguey, helping my father put stamps on packages," Perez recalls. "I play for factory team when Havana sign me. I was shortstop...only 155 pounds."

His nickname then was Flaco, which is Spanish for skinny. The Reds plucked him out of Cuba just before Castro told the U.S. where to get off. Perez was home in 1963, never to return until he finagled a visit with his mother and father in 1972. "They no want to leave Cuba, they want to die there," Tony says.

The Reds turned Tony into a third baseman, but his erratic throwing arm eventually landed him at first base, where he is stationed now. But, Cincinnati wanted to trade him last winter so they could have Dan Driessen play regularly at first. Driessen played third during the 1973 season, but mostly did an imitation of a croquet wicket as ball after ball rolled through his legs.

Cuban pitcher Mike Cuellar hoped his Baltimore Orioles would get Perez. Instead, the Orioles obtained Lee May from Houston and Cuellar called Perez. "Geez, I hoped we could get you, Tony," said Cuellar.

"That's all right," said Perez. "When you got May, you got my brother."

And, the Reds kept Perez, a most fortuitous happenstance.

From spring training to Riverfront Stadium

SPRING SHARPENING--
Dave Concepcion (top
photo) and Tony Perez
(bottom shot) sharpen their
fielding skills in spring
training.

COGS IN THE MACHINE-- Joe Morgan dives back to first against Steve Garvey and the Los Angeles Dodgers in top photo. Below, Alex Grammas and Sparky Anderson ponder strategy on the Reds bench.

BITES THE DUST-- Rookie Doug Flynn comes plowing into home against the Montreal Expos in top shot; below, Johnny Bench and pitching coach Larry Shepard confer with hurler Don Gullett.

FRED NORMAN

SPOT STARTER-- Clay Kirby, who was 10-6 for the Reds in '75, was used as both an occasional starter and a reliever.

THE BRAIN TRUST

JOHNNY BENCH

PETE ROSE AND GEORGE FOSTER

MVP

THE BIG GUNS-- The Big
Red Machine was fueled by
the strong hitting of the
men featured on this page.
George Foster, top photo,
bloomed into a slugger
when he moved into left
field for the Reds; Pete
Rose, Joe Morgan, Tony
Perez, Dave Concepcion
and Johnny Bench served
as the heart of the offense.

DON GULLETT

TAKING ADVANTAGE OF THE BREAK-- The '75 Reds seldom failed to take advantage of a good break. Danny Driessen makes good on a surprise steal, right; Bill Plummer waits out the oppositions pitcher, below right; the bottom photo shows what may have been the best break the Reds got all year -- Gary Nolan's return to the mound gave Cincinnati the extra starter the club needed.

PITCHING,POWER AND DE-FENSE--Jack Billingham, the veteran righthander on the Reds staff, above; some of the key hits in '75 came from Cincinnati reserves like Bill Plummer and Merv Retten-mund, upper right photo; the Reds defense was bolstered by the four Golden Glovers in photo on right; from the left they are, Dave Concepcion, Johnny Bench, Cesar Geronimo and Joe Morgan.

SAFE OR OUT? -- Pete Rose looks questionly as Johnny Bench makes the tag.

DAVE   CONCEPCION

chapter nine

There were close to 500 bleary-eyed sports journalists chasing the touring carnival called the 1975 World Series. A chartered Delta Boeing 707 full of them departed Cincinnati at 3 a.m. after Game Five, arriving at the nation's bean and schrod capital at 4:30 a.m., tired but smiling, their spirits lifted by liquid spirits at 30,000 feet.

A confused bus driver changed their attitude quickly when he managed to turn a 20-minute ride from Logan airport into a 60-minute ordeal.

The bussie stopped at red lights...and stopped at green lights, waiting for them to turn red. He wandered in and out of Boston's Combat Zone, the city's porno and prostitution strip. He weaved through Chinatown's streets, forcing writers to finally disembark a couple of blocks from the

Statler-Hilton with some angry expletives aimed his way, their suitcases and typewriters dragging behind them.

Once in the hotel, the weary typewriter jockeys discovered "their reserved room" had been sold out from under them and many spent a few hours in parlor rooms on rollaway beds. A few more expletives were deposited upon the stunned night clerk.

"You'd think these Boston people thought we were the Cincinnati Reds instead of a bunch of harmless writers," said Chicago's Jerome Holtzman.

The Cincinnati Reds were snug between the covers of their beds in the Howard Johnson's across the street, where Johnny Bench kiddingly said, "I'm so confident we'll wrap it up Saturday that I only brought one change of clothes."

Had he only known. It

would be four days before the next game. New England weather made the next few days a mid-fall night's nightmare.

Game Six could have been played on Friday, but that was an off-day. Both teams practiced, with Cincinnati's Jack Billingham scheduled to pitch Saturday against Bill Lee. On Saturday, the Reds awoke with rain pounding against their hotel room windows.

The Weatherman, encroaching upon the Governor's duties, granted the Boston Red Sox a temporary stay of execution. The "temporary stay of execution" words belong to Cincinnati's Joe Morgan. During Friday's workout, Morgan was told rain was predicted for Saturday. "If we get rained out, it'll just be a stay of execution for Boston. If we don't get 'em Saturday, we'll get 'em the next day."

CONFERENCE CLOSE UPS --The intensity of the World Series is reflected in these press conference close up shots of Sparky Anderson and Pete Rose (above), Darrel Johnson (below, left) and Fred Lynn (below right).

Said Pete Rose, "It's all over...next game. I'm a positive thinker. I've played 13 years and 2,000 games to get into this situation. I'm not concerned about when they'll play the seventh game, we'll win the sixth game."

The managers were playing games with their pitching selections as two inches of rain hit Boston Common and its environs.

"If we get rained out Sunday, Billingham is still my Game Six pitcher. Any Tuesday game, that belongs to Mr. Gullett. If we play Sunday and lose, Game Seven will be started by Gary Nolan, with Gullett ready to walk to the mound at a moment's notice," Cincinnati's Sparky Anderson promised.

Boston Manager Darrell Johnson, perhaps welcoming the rain, was just as certain. "Luis Tiant will pitch Game Seven. Lee and Tiant are my pitchers. The only thing that will change is if we get rained out Sunday and Monday. Then, Tiant pitches Game Six and Lee Game Seven."

It was still raining Sunday...no game again. Sparky Anderson decided to find a place for his athletes to ease the rust off and chose Tufts university in Medford, causing some scrambling among writers looking for rainy day stories.

A cab driver assured four writers in pursuit of the Reds that, "Sure, it's a short haul from the Statler-Hilton to Tufts." Paul Revere's ride was shorter. The meter clicked at $12.60 when the taxi jerked to a halt in front of Dussault (Ding) Cage fieldhouse, home of the Tufts Jumbos.

"I had my choice between Tufts and Harvard," said Sparky. "Harvard was too radical for my blood. I never thought I'd get into any university, let alone Tufts."

The workout brainstorm struck Sparky Sunday morning after the postponement and he asked Traveling Secretary Paul Campbell to round up all the players he could. Joe Morgan, Cesar Geronimo and Clay Kirby were never found.

The Reds rode to Fenway park to put on their uniforms, half expecting the ground crew to be atop the 37-foot high left field wall to escape water lapping at the 35-foot level. After dressing, they reboarded the bus and set sail (almost the correct word) for Tufts. The driver knew how to find Plymouth Rock, but not Tufts, so Sparky told him to stop at a gas station.

Wearing his road gray uniform and a red jacket with ''Cincinnati''

RAIN TALK-- Pete Rose does his best to give the press something to write about during one of the many rainy day press conferences.

emblazoned across the front, Sparky accosted the attendant with, ''How do we get to Tufts?'' Pitcher Will McEnaney leaned from a window and yelled, ''Ask him how to get to Fenway park, that'll blow his mind.'' As Sparky headed back for the bus, dashing through rain drops, Johnny Bench said, ''That station attendant has to be asking, 'OK, where's the Candid Camera?' '' It took another stop at a gas station and a pause at a bakery before the Reds reached their goal.

The Tufts Cage, as the locals call it, is a mammoth red brick barn structure. The floor is hard Tartan, a running track winding around it. Netting hangs from the roof and surrounds the gym, giving about 150 feet down each line. ''Reminds me of Wrigley field,'' Nolan grinned.

The pitchers threw from a plywood platform and were protected by a lacrosse goal. There was a standing room only crowd of media persons and stunned Tufts students, never expecting to see the Cincinnati Reds on their campus on a rainy Sunday morn.

''This is a good gimmick,'' said Sparky. ''It enables our guys to have some fun . . . they're enjoying this. It's better than sitting around watching it rain. It's just a trick I'm using to keep them busy.''

Nolan wasn't so sure how ''fun'' it was. ''Oh, yeah. It broke up the routine. But all I got done was a little catch, a little pepper and a hell of a lot of autograph signing. They must not have a sellout at Fenway if they have to promote the game by

NOLAN'S REVIEW -- ''Reminds me of Wrigley field,'' Gary Nolan said of the workout area at Tufts University.

sending us out to this college."

Eventually, the students got into the swing of things, serenading the Reds with chants of "Loo-ie, Loo-ie." Johnny Bench was standing in front of a basketball goal, palming a basketball for picture-hungry photographers. "Try to stuff it and kill yourself," suggested one student. Even Bench laughed.

One guy was having no fun at all. Easy-going Jack Billingham, the man with the perma-press smile, sat on the gym's floor, his back against a brick wall. The night before, Anderson decided to change pitching plans. He called Billingham and Nolan together after breakfast Sunday morning, informing them that Nolan, not Billingham, would pitch Game Six.

"Yes, I'm upset," said Billingham. "What could I do? I sat there and steamed a little bit when he told me. Like Sparky always does, he said a few extra words that were supposed to make me smile, but I didn't feel much like smiling."

Somebody suggested that maybe Billingham's plight fell under the category of "Taking One For The Club." Replied Billingham, "I've taken my share already. He's the boss and it is his decision. I have to abide by it, but I don't have to like it. I came to Boston expecting to pitch. I pitched here last weekend because of my sinker ball that makes it tough to hit balls over that Big Green Monster in left. Sparky held Nolan back then so he would pitch in Riverfront, so why not pitch me this time?"

Why was it done? Here's how Sparky explained it to Billingham: "I want you, Jack, as my long right handed relief pitcher because you have pitched relief before. Nolan has never pitched relief. Fred Norman will be my long relief left handed pitcher."

Billingham answered that one with, "We have relief pitchers, good ones. I can do it, but I really don't think the move was necessary."

A writer asked Nolan if he thought he could keep baseballs from flying out of Fenway, especially after Sparky said the week before that was the reason Nolan didn't pitch here the first two games. "If you are asking, 'Do I have a sinker?,' No, I don't have a sinker. I'm not gonna come all apart over Sparky's decision. I hope to take

UNHAPPY FIREMAN-- "Yes, I'm upset," Jack Billingham said shortly after he found out that he wasn't starting game six. "What could I do? I sat there and steamed a little bit when he told me."

advantage of it. I wasn't surprised because I've learned to keep an open mind about everything in baseball...if you can.

"I came here to play in a World Series, not sight-see. I might walk out there and pitch a shutout," Nolan concluded.

He wasn't going to walk out there Monday. Neither was Billingham or Gullett. The only guys who walked on Fenway park's soaked sod Monday were Baseball Commissioner Bowie Kuhn and his entourage. They stood in centerfield, up to their argyles in water, for 45 minutes as the rain pelted down on Monday afternoon before they decided the field was unplayable for Monday night.

As windshield wipers continued to be the most functional commodity in Boston Monday, Anderson held his muddy ground...Nolan on Tuesday and Gullet on Wednesday if there was a Game Seven.

Once again, the Reds motored to Tufts and this time Billingham was a noteworthy absentee, along with reserve Darrel Chaney. "We didn't think there'd be a workout on the day of the game and we didn't hear about the postponement," Chaney explained. Actually, Anderson scheduled the workout before the postponement was announced because he knew even if the game were played, there would be no batting practice.

Billingham and Chaney were driving around Boston in a rental car with their wives. At Tufts, Sparky was asked about their whereabouts and said, "Billingham is mad because he's not pitching." He smiled when he said it.

At Boston, Bill Lee was upset, too. Tiant would now pitch Game Six and if there

THE FOOLER--Luis Tiant's sweeping motion and variety of pitches carried him to an 18-14 record for the Red Sox during the regular season of '75. He completed 18 of the 35 games he started for Boston.

was a Game Seven, Lee would pitch that one. El Tiante, of course, was 2-0 in the Series. His presence, though, didn't frighten Morgan.

"The more I see of Tiant, the better I will hit him," Morgan promised. "Sure, he shut us out the first game (6-0), but we scored four the second time (Game Four, 5-4) and should have scored more." Morgan conveniently forgot that Cincinnati scored four off Tiant in Riverfront stadium. In Fenway, El Tiante hadn't allowed an earned run in 36 innings and no kind of run in 10 innings.

"Hey, Tiant is not a Tom Seaver," Morgan added. "He can't crank up a game on a night when he has nothing. Look at his record. He was 18-14 this season. That's enough to tell you he can't scare a team like we have."

Tiant and some of the other Red Sox were fighting colds, most of them obtained during Game Two in Boston, playing in a rousing rainstorm.

Boston right fielder Dwight Evans revealed the illnesses at a Monday afternoon press conference in front of news-starved journalists. They pursued it to the point of ludicrousness.

"How sick are you, Dwight?"

"I've played sick before, most players have," Evans said.

"Are you taking medication?"

"Yes," he shrugged.

"What kind, how often and what color are the pills?"

Obviously, if there wasn't a game Tuesday, the writers would soon be interviewing each other.

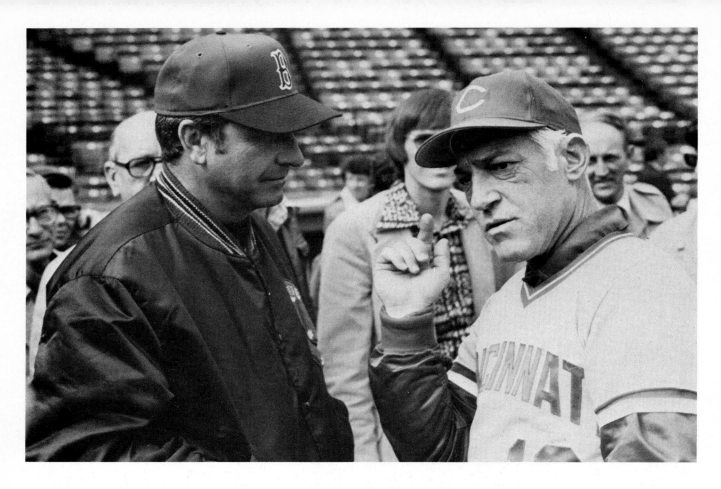

"NOW THIS IS THE WAY IT'S DONE"-- Sparky
Anderson explains a point to Darrell Johnson.

GETTING TOGETHER--Rawly Eastwick (left) and George Plimpton
discuss Series pitching in the Reds
clubhouse (above); the two second
sackers in the Series, Denny Doyle and
Joe Morgan, go over the playing
conditions at Fenway (below).

CUBAN POWER--The two
Cuban superstars of the Series,
Luis Tiant and Tony Perez, go at
it head-to-head.

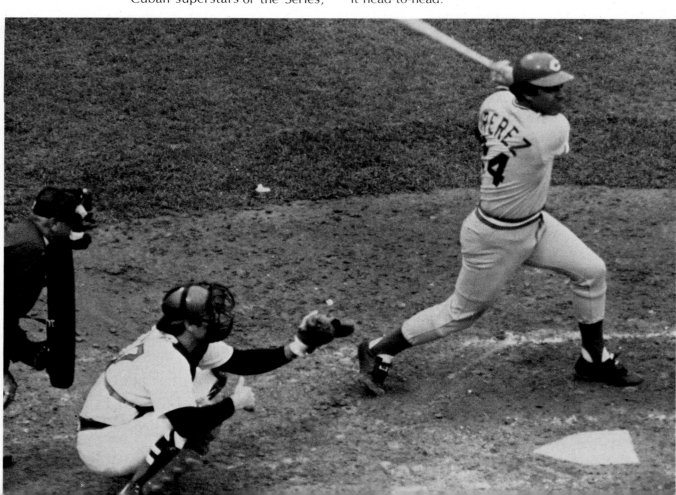

chapter ten

When the Cincinnati Reds are in Chicago, the same bus driver always transports them from O'Hare Airport to the Executive House Hotel, and on the round trips to and from Wrigley Field.

The guy is so enamored with his assignment that he carefully places a sign in the lower right corner of the windshield. The sign, in script red, says, "Cincinnati Reds." One time in June, the team bus was rumbling down Michigan Avenue when it came to a halt at a traffic light behind Chicago Transit Authority bus 1720.

Suddenly, although the light had turned green and cars were honking, the driver swung open his doors and ran back to the Cincinnati bus. When he arrived, the team driver flipped open his doors to find out what was wrong. "You guys go all the way this year...I'm with ya," the guy yelled into the door. Then, he ran back to his bus and drove off.

Now, four months later, the Reds were one game away from giving that Chicago bus driver what he wanted, along with a few million other people in Southwestern Ohio, Northern Kentucky and Southern Indiana.

There was no doubt Game Six would finally be played on October 21, a Tuesday. The sun was shining all day and the sky was clear when the Reds awoke for breakfast.

Reserve catcher Bill Plummer sat nibbling at scrambled eggs, then lit a cigaret. Early in the season, Plummer gave up smoking and hadn't touched one until the World Series. "I'm up to five a day," he said. "It's all nerves, the suspense of this thing is driving me crazy. I just couldn't stand it. I'm not buying any yet, just bummin' a few here and there."

For the third time, the Reds were to face Luis Tiant, already 2-0 against them, and if El Tiante was nervous before the game, he kept it deep within his Cuban heart.

"I just want to prove one more time I can pitch," he said during batting practice. "There is no secret. I get them out, I stay. I no get them out, I go. I no want to be big hero, I just want to enjoy the game. I have been released twice. Big deal. If I hadn't made it with Boston, I would have played with Mexico City Tigers."

Cincinnati's Tony Perez walked past and spotted El Tiante encircled by writers. "Hey, quijada, quit talking so much," Perez yelled. A Spanish writer translated quijada...jaws. Somebody asked him about his cold and Tiant said it was fine, thank you, he had taken some - - - -.

Depending upon which newspaper you read, Tiant took "serum or syrup or cereal." Those are the three different words the newsmen scribbled in their notebooks, their translations of the Spanish-accented word Tiant mumbled.

There were 35,205 payees in Fenway Park, plus a few hardy adventurers who had climbed billboards outside the park and were perched on top, peering over the left field wall.

They were about to see one of the finest baseball games offered the public in the history of the World Series, an action-stuffed panorama that lasted four hours and one minute...the one minute sending Bostonians into a frenzy.

Tiant began shakily. Pete Rose slammed a line drive to left, a prospective base hit - - except Carl Yastrzemski was out there again. Yaz skidded on his knees and made the catch. Rose saluted him with a tip of his cap.

Loo-ie walked Ken Griffey on a full count, then went to 3-and-1 on Joe Morgan before Morgan foul-popped to the catcher. The inning ended with Johnny Bench striking out.

Gary Nolan was not so fortunate. All the elements of a great story were there. The guy who missed baseball for 2½ years

VICTORY LAP--Luis Tiant trots around Fenway as his fans, includin those atop the billboard, chant out, "Loo-ie, Loo-ie.

THREE QUICK ONES--"Cecil Cooper (above) a n d Denny Doyle were retired easily. Yaz poked a single to right, Carlton Fisk poked a single to left and Fred Lynn (crossing plate below) punctured a 420 foot homer..."

coming back to win the final game of the World Series after stunning even his manager with 15 regular season victories.

Cecil Cooper and Denny Doyle were retired easily. Yaz poked a single to right, Carlton Fisk poked a single to left and Fred Lynn punctured a 420-foot homer to right center and just like that, the Red Sox were in front, 3-0.

Nolan retired the next four without a whimper, striking out two, but when Boston came to bat in the third, Nolan was gone and Fred Norman was in. It was to be the start of a Pitching Parade as Cincinnati Manager Sparky Anderson used, in order: Nolan, Norman, Jack Billingham, Clay Carroll, Pedro Borbon, Rawly Eastwick, Will McEnaney and Pat Darcy. At game's end, only Clay Kirby and Don Gullett were left. Kirby warmed up, but Gullett was Sparky's ace for a possible Game Seven.

Tiant settled down for the next three innings with that 3-0 lead, working himself out of a minor dilemma in the fourth when shortstop Rick Burleson's error put runners on first and third with two outs. But, Dave Concepcion popped to first baseman Cecil Cooper in foul territory.

Finally, the Reds rid themselves of the ghost of Luis Tiant. It took some doing, and some patience by Boston Manager Darrell Johnson.

The Reds tied the game, 3-3, in the fifth. With one out, pinch-hitter Ed Armbrister walked, Pete Rose singled and Ken Griffey smashed a 2-2 pitch to left center for a two-run triple, scoring on Johnny Bench's single off the wall.

At 3-3, Johnson wasn't about to lift Tiant, the New England deity. Cincinnati's

Anderson, though, continued his parade. Billingham, the man shuffled aside in favor of Nolan to start this game, came on in the third with two outs and the bases loaded to strike out Rico Petrocelli. In the fourth, Dwight Evans doubled and Rick Burleson walked on four straight pitches. Tiant bunted the runners up a base, then Billingham retired Cecil Cooper and Denny Doyle on meek grounders to wriggle free and earn some personal vengeance.

The groans could be heard all over the Back Bay in the seventh when pesky Ken Griffey opened with a single and Joe Morgan duplicated. Tiant sloughed aside Cincinnati's two most dangerous RBI men, Johnny Bench and Tony Perez on fly balls.

George Foster did what Bench and Perez couldn't do, slamming a Tiant fast ball off the wall for a two-run double. When Cesar Geronimo said hello to Tiant in the eighth with a home run to right, Johnson pulled Tiant. The score was Cincinnati 6, Boston 3 - - and the Reds were six outs away from their first World Series championship in 35 years. But, the Fenway Park fans rose and gave Tiant a stadium-shaking ovation as he disappeared into the dugout.

The Red Sox would not fall down and die in front of the functioning Big Red Machine. No way. Pedro Borbon began the eighth inning and Fred Lynn drove a single off Borbon's right shin.

On a 3-and-2 pitch, Borbon walked Rico Petrocelli. It was time for Anderson to shut off this nonsense - - come in with his best, Rawly Eastwick - - the man who already owned two victories and a save in this Series.

Eastwick struck out Dwight Evans and retired Rick Burleson on a screamer to shallow left.

Now, the Reds were four outs away from diamond rings and $21,000 checks. Bernie Carbo, once a Cincinnati Red and already the owner of one pinch-hit homer in the Series, had different ideas when Darrell Johnson sent him to bat.

Eastwick took him to 2-and-2 and threw a good inside fast ball. Somehow, with a freak swing, Carbo fouled it. ''I was fighting everything off inside,'' Bernie said. ''I didn't want to strike out. That wild swing was kind of embarrassing, a Japanese swing, but it WAS a strike.''

The next pitch was immediately ticketed for a Disaster Area, said Eastwick. ''A lousy pitch, a high fast ball.'' Carbo bludgeoned it to dead center, into the bleachers more than

HELLO-- ''Cesar Geronimo said hello to Tiant in the eighth with a home run to right.''

420 feet away. It was a 6-6 tie after Bernie made his triumphant circle around the bases, arms above his head.

"I almost hated to do it," Carbo said. "Sparky Anderson is the reason I'm playing big league baseball. But, my greatest thrill would be to win a World Series...and I'd rather it be me on the winning side than him. I played in the minors for Sparky and I needed to be pushed. I've never had a manager work so hard with me as Sparky did. He had me out every day at 10 a.m. and worked with me...batting practice and fielding. Then, after a game, he would get a couple of coaches to work a couple more hours. Man, he pushed me."

Carbo played in the 1970 World Series for Cincinnati, won by Baltimore. "Funny, my first hit in the big leagues was a home run." Carbo's first hit in the 1975 World Series was a homer in Game Three in Cincinnati off his ex-roomie Clay Carroll. As he passed Pete Rose at third base that night, he said, "Don't you wish you were that strong?"

After the homer in Game Six, a blow that tied that game, 6-6, Carbo didn't say a word to old buddy Pete. He knew Rose would be too downhearted.

The Red Sox tried to end it in the bottom of the ninth, but left fielder Foster quickly unended it with a daring, dazzling play. If the Reds had won this game,

Foster's catch would have been the one the world talked about instead of the one Dwight Evans would later make.

Boston filled the bases with none out - - and incredibly didn't score. Fred Lynn lobbed a fly ball to shallow left, right down the line that runs within three feet of a high wall protruding dangerously close to the field.

Foster thought briefly about letting the ball drop, hoping it would plop foul. If he caught it, Denny Doyle might score from third base. Foster, running full bore, was fearful he might catch the baseball, but crash into the wall and not be able to make a throw.

"I was afraid it might be fair (it was ruled fair by umpire Dick Stello)," said Foster. "To be sure, I caught it." Boston third base coach Don Zimmer says he was yelling to Doyle, "Don't go, you can't go...no, no, no." Doyle thought he said, "Go, go, go," and ran--to his death. Foster, with a near pin-point peg, eradicated him at home in a funnel of dust for a double play. Will McEnaney retired Rico Petrocelli on a grounder to Rose, leaving the game at 6-6 and turning Game Six into the second extra-inning game of the 1975 World Series.

THE MAN WHO DID THE DAMAGE--Bernie Carbo stands near the outfield scoreboard in Fenway Park after he hit his dramatic three run homer in game six of the Series.

It was Cincinnati's turn in the 11th and 12th to bring Bostonians' hearts to their mouths. Pete Rose was brushed with a pitch leading off the 11th and Ken Griffey forced him with a weak bunt on which catcher Carlton Fisk made a Johnny Bench-type throw to second. Joe Morgan dispatched a liner toward right, near the 380 mark. Evans made a leaping stab before falling against the wall, recovered and made a throw that ended up doubling Griffey off first.

"I don't know how I made the catch," said Evans. "There was no time to think. Yogi Berra always said you can't think and hit at the same time. It's the same with defense. You can't think and make good plays at the same time. Somebody said I hit the wall, but I don't remember it. The less you think about something like that, the better off you are."

Morgan said when he hit the ball, he gave Evans a chance to catch it. "I had top spin on it, so I knew it would sink," he said. "I was hoping it would go over his head, but he was playing deeper and more toward right than he has in the other games. I don't understand why."

In the 12th, Tony Perez and George Foster singled with one out, but Rick Wise, making his first relief showing since 1973, coaxed a fly ball from Dave Concepcion and struck out Cesar Geronimo, looking at an inside fast ball.

The game was four hours old when Carlton Fisk dug his spikes into the batter's box, hitched up his pants, and pointed his bat at Cincinnati pitcher Pat Darcy, who had retired six straight in the 10th and 11th.

Darcy's first pitch was ball one. The next pitch...well, it touched off pandemonium. Fisk swung

DOYLE GUNNED DOWN -- Denny Doyle was tagged out at the plate in Series action at Boston.

and it arched high into the New England skies.

After swinging the bat, Fisk froze near the batter's box, a couple steps toward first, watching the majestic flight of the baseball as it soared toward the ugly Green Monster that protects Lansdowne Street down the left field line.

Fisk's arms were spread wide, pleading, a silent prayer to the baseball gods. "Stay fair, stay fair. It's either foul or off the foul pole for a homer. Stay fair, please."

Fisk's request was answered. The ball thudded against the tall gold pole, 315 feet from the plate and 55 feet above the ground. Home run...Boston wins, 7-6, sending the World Series to a dramatic and climactic seventh game.

The blow was administered at 12:34 a.m., and an estimated 70 million people were still watching at home on TV. It was four hours and one minute after the game's first pitch.

"It was a low pitch that sailed away," pitcher Pat Darcy said later. "I tried to throw it too hard. I overthrew. I knew it would curve foul or hit the foul pole."

When it struck the pole, some of the 35,205 fans, most of them delirious, spilled onto the field as Fisk circled the bases, weaving in and out of fans, shaking hands with many. "I was making sure I touched every base. If I had to straight-arm fans, push people out of the way or knock them down, I was going to touch them all."

Ironically, Sport Magazine, which presents a car to the World Series MVP every year, had taken a vote of some sports writers during the eighth inning with Cincinnati ahead, 6-3.

The winner was Cincinnati relief pitcher Rawly

129

Eastwick, who didn't even own a car. Then, Rawly was ripped by Bernie Carbo in the eighth for the three-run homer that tied the game and Sport Magazine's Dick Schaap tore up the results.

With Game Seven coming up, the MVP might be any number of players from either team. One of the prospects, should the Reds win, was Pete Rose.

It was nearly an hour after Game Six and many fans were still standing in the grandstands celebrating. Rose, who should have been morose after the Reds lost a chance to win the World Series that very night, was walking toward the Cincinnati bus. He stopped and glanced through a grandstand portal toward the field.

"If this isn't the number one pastime in America, I don't know what is," Rose said. "The Super Bowl will really have to come up with something to top this. This game had to be the greatest World Series game in history and I'm just glad I'll be able to say I was in it. My son and I will be talking about this one for a long time to come."

Those words came from a guy whose team had just lost one of its biggest games of 1975. But, there WAS a tomorrow.

GAME SIX STARS--Dwight Evans snags Joe Morgan's line shot (above); Carlton Fisk is greeted by his teammates after his foul pole homer.

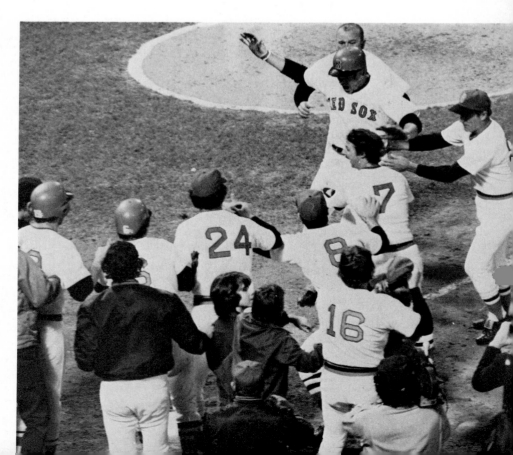

AFTER THE SIXTH--Rose explained to reporters how much the sixth game of the Series would help the popularity of baseball (above); Pat Darcy (below, right) and Rawly Eastwick (below, left) contemplate the gopher balls they tossed in the game.

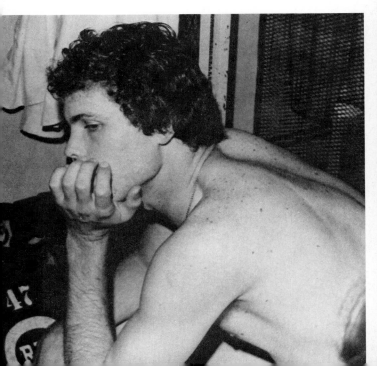

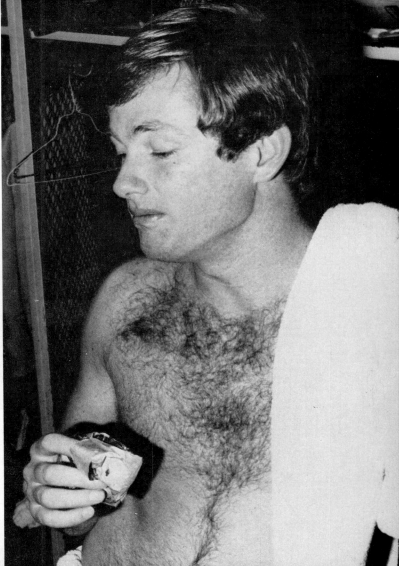

END OF THE LINE -- The 1975 baseball season came down to this final game of the Series. Above, the Reds line up for the National Anthem; Bill Lee hurls a frisbee into the stands, right; The line-ups for both teams are posted on the scoreboard, below; and George Foster gets tossed out at second during the game.

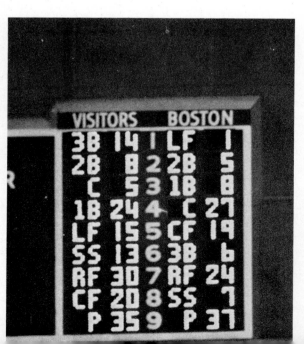

VISITORS		BOSTON	
3B	14 1	LF	1
2B	8 2	2B	5
C	5 3	1B	8
1B	24 4	C	27
LF	15 5	CF	19
SS	13 6	3B	6
RF	30 7	RF	24
CF	20 8	SS	7
P	35 9	P	37

chapter eleven

There was a full moon on Wednesday night, October 22, a perfect omen for Boston's Space Man, pitcher Bill Lee. On some days, Lee slips into a track suit and runs to the ball park from a Back Bay subway station. On other days, he rides a bicycle.

On this important day in his life, Lee turned conventional and rode in by car. He wasn't conventional before the game, though, as newspapermen swarmed around him.

Spotting a young lady with a baby seated in the stands, Lee walked over and planted a kiss on the youngster's pate. "As soon as I throw my hat in the ring, they'll know I'm running for office," said Lee, who spends Sunday mornings before games playing flag football.

By contrast, Cincinnati pitcher Don Gullett, a shy guy, hid in the shelter of the Reds' clubhouse, off-limits to media folks before a game.

Earlier in the week, Lee read in the newspapers that Cincinnati Manager Sparky Anderson said Gullett was on a direct course to Cooperstown and the Baseball Hall of Fame.

"The way I got it figured," said Lee, "is that right after this game, Gullett goes straight to the Hall of Fame and I go directly to Eliot's Lounge across the street."

As usual, the single-decked Fenway park was stuffed with humanity for this seventh and final game, 35,205 paying fans--and some added starters. Several adventuresome youths used a rope to scale the perpendicular outer wall of Fenway, coming over the top near the center field bleachers.

After a precarious walk along the narrow wall, they plopped into the stands and disappeared among the paying populace. Others scaled the scoreboard atop the right field bleachers and sat there all night.

They were all ready for an exciting climax to an already thrilling World Series.

Lee easily retired the Reds in the first. Gullett gave up a leadoff double to Bernie Carbo, whose Game Six heroics earned him a start in left field for Game Seven. Carbo managed to reach third, but died there when Gullett struck out Carlton Fisk.

With one out in the second, George Foster struck a blow off The Green Monster and made the mistake of trying to turn it into a double. Sure, Carl Yastrzemski wasn't out there. But, Carbo played the carom perfectly and easily caught Foster at second.

Once again, Boston put its leadoff man on base to begin its second when Gullett walked Fred Lynn. He remained anchored at first as Gullett pushed aside three straight Bosox.

Ken Griffey led off Cincinnati's third with a single, but Cesar Geronimo bounced into a doubleplay. Something had to happen soon if both teams kept putting their leadoff hitters on base.

It happened in the Boston third, in a big way. Once again Gullett walked the leadoff hitter, Carbo. Denny Doyle singled to right. Yaz punched a single to right and Carbo sped home as Fenway park rocked. Yaz had taken second on a throw home, so Carlton Fisk was walked intentionally, filling the bases with nobody out.

Gullett forced Fred Lynn to look at a third strike, then completely lost his composure. The little lefthander with the white-hot fast ball walked Rico Petrocelli on a full count, forcing in Doyle, then walked Dwight Evans, forcing in Yaz.

Now, it was 3-0 and Cincinnati Manager Sparky Anderson remained entrenched in the dugout. During the season, four walks and two hits in one inning were unheard of because Sparky never let a pitcher last that long. But, Don Gullett is something special to Sparky Anderson.

His patience was rewarded when Gullett worked out of the mess by striking out Rick Burleson and Bill Lee. But, it was 3-0. If the Cincinnati Reds were to be 1975 world champions, they would have to do it the same way they had done it all year, by coming from behind.

With the full moon at his back, Lee kept tempting a horrible disaster. Joe Morgan led off the fourth with a bunt single and stole second. He moved no further

BIG OUTS IN THE SEVENTH GAME-- Ken Griffey is one-half of an important double play (above); Fred Lynn looked at a called third strike and then looked at the umpire.

as Johnny Bench, Tony Perez and George Foster, Cincinnati's Guillotine Guys, all popped up.

Dave Concepcion led off the fifth with an infield hit and Ken Griffey reached on Denny Doyle's error--two on, none out. Was now the time? Nope, Cesar Geronimo struck out and pinch-hitter Merv Rettenmund slashed into a 6-4-3 doubleplay. Maybe that full moon was keeping Lee alive. It was still 3-0 after five and the Red Sox were rid of Gullett. Rettenmund batted for Gullett in the fifth.

Jack Billingham, the maligned starter turned relief pitcher, loaded the bases in the Boston fifth but escaped as more than 75 million TV viewers wondered how long pitchers could keep sticking their necks in nooses and pulling them back out in the nick of time.

For the fourth straight inning, Lee put the leadoff man on base when Pete Rose ripped a single to right. Joe Morgan flied to right. Johnny Bench grounded to shortstop and Rick Burleson's throw to second forced Rose. But, Denny Doyle's throw toward first for an attempted doubleplay was wild and Bench was safe.

Still, there were two outs and Lee appeared safe again, but he tried to play it cute.

On his second pitch to Tony Perez, Lee offered a lollipop, a hump-backed blooper, a changeup. Perez was no sucker. He timed it perfectly. The ball was last seen disappearing into the New England darkness, still rising as it sailed past a light standard in left center, a two-run homer that brought the Reds to within 3-2.

''I looked for it,'' said Perez. ''He throw it to me in the fourth inning. I tell guys in the dugout if he throw it again, I hit it out of park.''

The Reds drew even in the seventh at 3-3 when Lee walked Ken Griffey on four pitches, then left the game with a blister of second-degree burn proportions. Roger Moret replaced him and Griffey pilfered second, scoring on Rose's single up the middle.

Billingham and Clay Carroll were keeping the Red Sox silent through eight innings--and now it was the ninth, a 3-3 tie as the Reds came to bat.

Jim Burton was Boston's pitcher and he walked Griffey on a 3-and-2 count, the fourth time Griffey was aboard this game and the 13th time during the Series. Cesar Geronimo bunted

OUT OF A JAM -- ''Jack Billingham, the maligned starter turned relief pitcher, loaded the bases in the Boston fifth but escaped...''

Kenny to second, but pinch-hitter Dan Driessen grounded out, sending Griffey to third and bringing up Rose.

"I would have liked a base hit, of course," said Rose. "But I had never faced Burton and it's tough for me to hit a pitcher the first time I've seen him. I was hoping for a walk so I could leave it up to our MVP man, Joe Morgan." Like Griffey, Rose walked on a 3-and-2.

Morgan agreed with the Rose "walk" theory.

"I was hoping Pete would walk," said Morgan. "He has had so many clutch hits in this Series I was afraid he might have run out of them."

Morgan fouled a couple pitches, then rainbowed a blooper to center, scoring Griffey with the most important run of 1975--a 4-3 Cincinnati lead.

"A couple of years ago I would have struck out on that pitch," said Morgan. "It was a good pitch, a sailing fast ball down and away. But, I'm a better hitter than I was two years ago. I would have pulled off the pitch two years ago. Sure, it was a blooper, but I could have

THE SHOT THAT SHOOK NEW ENGLAND-- "On his second pitch to Tony Perez, Lee offered a lollipop, a hump-backed blooper, a changeup... the ball was last seen disappearing into the New England darkness......."
The arrow points to the ball in flight.

been the hero in Game Six with that line drive Dwight Evans caught against the fence, so I don't feel bad about this one being a blooper.''

It wasn't over yet, of course. The 35,205 stayed riveted, praying their Red Sox had yet another miracle up their double knits for the bottom of the ninth.

''I just told 'em to bring in Will McEnaney for the ninth and it's all over,'' said Morgan. ''Will is my man. I have super confidence in him. I thought, 'No way they'd get a run off Will.' ''

Sparky Anderson answered Morgan's request by sending the 23-year-old lefty to the mound, some kind of pressure for a rookie.

Quickly, pinch-hitters Juan Beniquez and Bob Montgomery were retired. Now, McEnaney was facing Carl Yastrzemski.

''When I was a kid, I watched Yaz on TV,'' said McEnaney. ''Then, I would go out in the backyard of my Springfield, O., home and imagine striking him out to end the World Series. I never dreamed I would actually be facing him as the last out of the real World Series.

''I won't lie. Man, I was scared. I didn't want to walk him, not with Carlton Fisk coming up next,'' Mac said. The script changed ever-so-slightly. McEnaney did not strike out Yaz.

Yaz popped a fly to medium center. The fans prayed, ''Drop it, man, drop it. Please, please drop it.'' Center fielder Cesar Geronimo was so sure he leaped in the air and did a jig as the ball descended. Then, he caught it. McEnaney raced to home plate and leaped into the arms of Johnny Bench.

The Cincinnati Reds, for the first time in 35 years, were baseball's king of the mountain.

For years, in any idle ear, the Cincinnati Reds insisted, unequivocally, that they were the best baseball team in the world. But the Oakland A's, New York Mets and Los Angeles Dodgers kept making liars out of them. Chit-chat champions. Paper Tigers.

The vindication arrived for 1975 at 11:22 p.m., October 22, 1975. Under a full moon. In Fenway Park.

One slender run, that run scored on Morgan's blooper hit, was the difference over seven games. One skinny run. It was apropos. The World Series was that close.

Before the final game, Bill Lee had said, ''It's a shame we have to play the final game. These two teams are so close they should call off Game Seven, declare co-champions and stage a picnic here tonight.''

It was also oh-so-apropos the way the Reds put Game Seven together in a tidy package marked, ''Cincinnati Reds, Patented.''

This game was the 1975 season in microcosm, stuffed into one neat box. First, they spotted the Red

Will McEnaney retired three in a row to nail down the title.

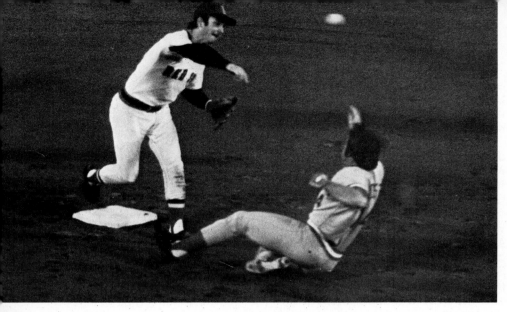

SLIDE WISE--Pete Rose, who knows how to make a hard slide count, did just that against the Red Sox and Denny Doyle in the seventh game of the Series.

Sox a 3-0 lead. Then, they came back to snatch it away on their last bat. It was the 51st time this season, counting Playoffs and World Series, that the Reds came from behind to win--close to half their 115 victories. It was the 30th time they won a game on their last at bat.

All the components functioned. Pete Rose used aggressiveness to ruin that Boston doubleplay attempt in the sixth, forcing second baseman Denny Doyle to throw into the dugout. Tony Perez followed with the homer that cut Boston's lead to 3-2.

"I went into second as hard as I could and as cleanly as I could," said Rose, using the word "cleanly" as a reminder to those who remember the 1973 National League playoffs against the Mets. In that one, Pete slid into Bud Harrelson, touching off a riot that earned Rose boos around the league for two years. "I didn't touch Doyle, but he must have jumped 10 feet in the air to avoid me and made the bad throw," Pete added.

Ken Griffey, one of Cincinnati's speed freaks, used speed to tie the game in the seventh, walking and stealing second. They used Rose's insatiable appetite for the clutch hit when Pete punched a single up the middle to score Griffey and tie it, 3-3.

Then, with everything on

the line, the man who did most for "baseball's best team," did it one more time. Morgan had two strikes and two outs staring him in the face, but lobbed a single to center, scoring Griffey.

In the raucous clubhouse, the champagne, beer and water cascaded over everybody's heads--friend or stranger--including the architect of The Big Red Machine, President Bob Howsam.

Howsam was standing on the fringes when Coach Alex Grammas approached him and asked, "Tell the truth, now. You were worried, weren't you, when we were down, 3-0?" Howsam grinned and managed a "yes." Then, Howsam walked over to pitcher Will McEnaney and rubbed his hand through Will's champagne-soaked hair. "Thanks," Howsam said.

"You're welcome, Mr. Howsam. I know how much this means to you," McEnaney answered.

"We've been saying for three years we have the best team in baseball," said catcher Johnny Bench. "Now, it's really something knowing that tomorrow we'll wake up and can say for the next few months that we're the champions."

Added Joe Morgan, "We have the best team in baseball, but never proved it on the field. We finally proved it. Now we can go home and say we're the best team in baseball and nobody can dispute it. This is something I've looked forward to for 11 years," he added. "Seven years ago, I was playing for Houston, fighting against New York to stay out of the cellar. It's been a long time coming."

Manager Sparky Anderson, the man who bore the brunt of the past failures and would have borne them again for some questionable

decisions in this Series, was eloquent, in his own way, about the 1975 World Series.

"In all sincerity, I don't think there has been a greater World Series," he said. "Boston can stand right up there with us. There were two great teams in this Series, but I think we proved this team can win big ball games. We deserved it for three years, we finally got it."

Clay Carroll, as always, was worth a few funny words. After getting credit for the victory, Carroll said, "Don't ask me too many questions. I don't answer questions, I just pitch." Later, Carroll ran up to pitcher Fred Norman and said excitedly, "Mr. Howsam said we're gonna have a carat in our championship rings!"

"What color?" asked Norman with a serious face.

"Didn't ask him," answered Carroll with a puzzled look. "Yellow I guess."

It could have been Joe

ALL EVEN--Ken Griffey comes racing home to tie the seventh game 3-3.

Morgan or Rawly Eastwick or Ken Griffey just as easily, but Pete Rose was named World Series Most Valuable Player. His reward was a new car, which he traded for a land rover jeep. He should share driving privileges with his teammates.

"I'd like to divide it up into 25 equal parts," Rose said. "This World Series has been fun. Joe Morgan is my favorite baseball player and Tony Perez is my favorite person." The first thing Rose did the next morning when he returned to Cincinnati was turn on his private videotape machine and watch Game Seven all over on a tape a friend made off the telecast.

All season long, Cincinnati radio announcer Marty Brennaman ended each game's broadcast the same way. On the game's last out that was a Cincinnati victory, Brennaman would say, "And this one belongs to the Reds."

At a post-Series private party, Johnny Bench stood in front of a microphone and gave an eloquent speech. At the conclusion, he drove the point home clearly by saying:

"And, if I may borrow a phrase from Marty Brennaman, THIS ONE BELONGS TO THE REDS."

THE BLOOPER THAT WON-- Joe Morgan slapped this pitch into centerfield, driving home the winning Series run for the Reds.

LET THE GOOD TIMES ROLL--In the World Champs clubhouse, Tony Perez and Johnny Bench flash victory smiles (above); Danny Driessen and Ed Armbrister offer each other congratulations (below).

CLUBHOUSE CLAMBAKE-- The Reds live it up after their Series win. Above, Pedro Borbon, Darrel Chaney and Doug Flynn do a little singing; below right, Bob Howsam and Joe Morgan explain that winning feeling to the press; below left, Don Gullett gets dunked in the bubbles.

world champs

SPOILS FOR THE VICTOR--Commissioner Bowie Kuhn (left) presents Sparky Anderson the World Championship trophy.

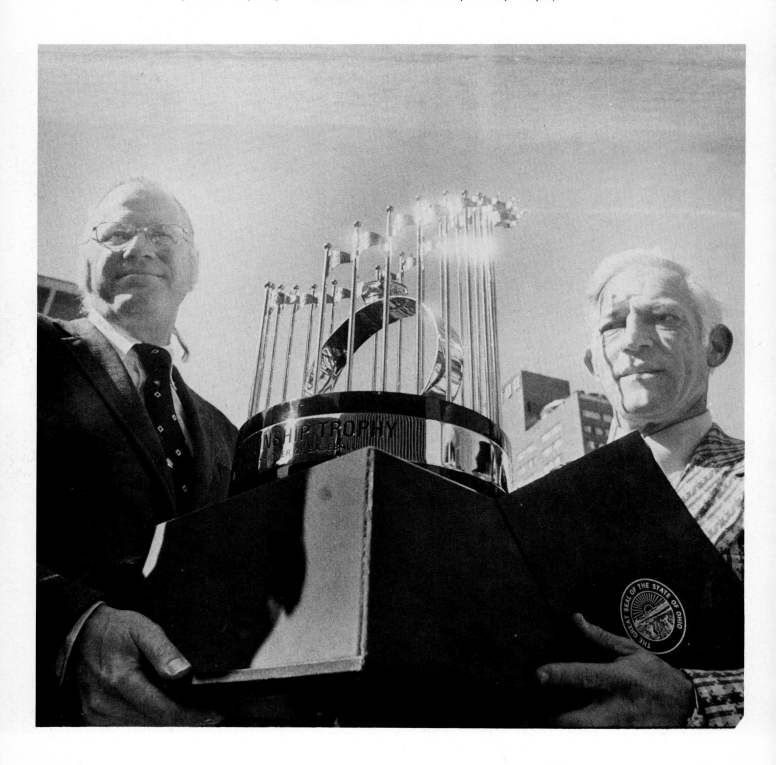

the
stats

1975
world series box scores

game 1

red sox 6, reds 0

CINCINNATI	ab	r	h	bi
Rose, 3b	4	0	0	0
Morgan, 2b	4	0	2	0
Bench, c	4	0	0	0
Perez, 1b	4	0	0	0
Foster, lf	4	0	2	0
Concepcion, ss	4	0	0	0
Griffey, rf	3	0	1	0
Geronimo, cf	1	0	0	0
Gullett, p	3	0	0	0
Carroll, p	0	0	0	0
McEnaney, p	0	0	0	0
Totals	31	0	5	0

BOSTON	ab	r	h	bi
Evans, rf	4	1	1	0
Doyle, 2b	3	1	2	0
Yastrzemski, lf	4	1	1	1
Fisk, c	3	1	0	1
Lynn, cf	4	0	2	0
Petrocelli, 3b	3	1	2	2
Burleson, ss	3	0	3	1
Cooper, 1b	3	0	0	1
Tiant, p	3	1	1	0
Totals	30	6	12	6

```
Cincinnati      000 000 000-0
Boston          000 000 60x-6
```

DP-Cincinnati 2. LOB-Cincinnati 6, Boston 9. 2B-Morgan, Petrocelli, Griffey. S-Doyle, Evans. SF-Cooper.

	ip	h	r	er	bb	so
Gullett [L, 0-1]	6	10	4	4	4	3
Carroll	0	0	1	1	1	0
McEnany	2	2	1	1	1	1
Tiant [W, 1-0]	9	5	0	0	2	3

Balk-Tiant
Time 2:25
Attendance 35,205

how the runs were scored

Red Sox Seventh -- Tiant led off inning by singling to left off Reds pitcher Don Gullett. Evans laid down a bunt which pitcher Gullett fielded and threw to second in an attempt to cut down the advancing runner. The throw was wild, ending up in the center field - both runners were safe, nobody out. Doyle singled to left, advancing Tiant to third and Evans to second. Yastrzemski singled to right, scoring Tiant and advancing Evans to third and Doyle to second. Score: Red Sox 1, Reds 0. Clay Carroll replaced Don Gullett as Reds pitcher. Fisk walked, scoring Evans and advancing Doyle to third and Yastrzemski to second. Score: Red Sox 2, Reds 0. Lynn struck out. Petrocelli singled to left, scoring Doyle and Yastrzemski. Red Sox 4, Reds 0. Burleson singled to left, scoring Fisk. Both runners advanced a base on the throw to the plate. Red Sox 5, Reds 0. Cooper hit a sacrifice fly to right, scoring Petrocelli and advancing Burleson to third. Red Sox 6, Reds 0. Tiant popped to third. 6 runs, 5 hits, 1 left.

game 2

reds 3, red sox 2

CINCINNATI	ab	r	h	bi
Rose, 3b	4	0	2	0
Morgan, 2b	3	1	0	0
Bench, c	4	1	2	0
T. Perez, 1b	3	0	0	1
G. Foster, lf	4	0	.1	0
Concepcion, ss	4	1	1	1
Griffey, rf	4	0	1	1
Geronimo, cf	3	0	0	0
Billingham, p	2	0	0	0
Borbon, p	0	0	0	0
McEnaney, p	0	0	0	0
Rettenmund, ph	1	0	0	0
Eastwick, p	1	0	0	0
Totals	33	3	7	3

BOSTON	ab	r	h	bi
Cooper, 1b	5	0	1	0
Doyle, 2b	4	0	1	0
Yastrzemski, lf	3	2	1	0
Fisk, c	3	0	1	1
Lynn, cf	4	0	0	0
Petrocelli, 3b	4	0	2	1
Evans, rf	2	0	0	0
Burleson, ss	4	0	1	0
Lee, p	3	0	0	0
Drago, p	0	0	0	0
Carbo, ph	1	0	0	0
Totals	33	2	7	2

```
Cincinnati      000 100 002-3
Boston          100 001 000-2
```

E. Concepcion. DP-Cincinnati 1. LOB-Cincinnati 6, Boston 8. 2B-Cooper, Bench, Griffey. SB-Concepcion.

	ip	h	r	er	bb	so
Billingham	5⅔	6	2	1	2	5
Borbon	⅓	0	0	0	0	0
McEnaney	1	0	0	0	0	2
Eastwick [W, 1-0]	2	1	0	0	1	1
Blee	8	5	2	2	2	5
Drago [L, 0-1]	1	2	1	1	0	0

HBP- by Billingham [Evans]. Time 2:38 Attendance 35,205

how the runs were scored

Red Sox first - Cooper led off inning by doubling to left off Reds pitcher Jack Billingham. Doyle picked up an infield hit, Cooper advancing to third. Yastrzemski forced Doyle at second, Billingham to Concepcion and Cooper is caught of third base and put out by Bench. Yastrzemski advances to second on the play at the plate. Fisk singled to right, scoring Yastrzemski. Score: Red Sox 1, Reds 0. Lynn is thrown out, Morgan to Perez. 1 run, 3 hits, 1 left.

Reds fourth - Rose was thrown out, Doyle to Cooper. Morgan drew a walk from Red Sox pitcher Bill Lee. Bench singled to center, advancing Morgan to third. Perez forced Bench at second, Burleson to Doyle, Morgan scoring on the play. Score: Red Sox 1, Reds 1. Foster singled to left, advancing Perez to second. Concepcion popped to center. 1 run, 2 hits, 2 left.

Red Sox sixth - Doyle was thrown out, Morgan to Perez. Yastrzemski singled to right. Concepcion booted a roller off bat of Fisk, Yastrzemski advances to second, both runners safe. Lynn popped to right. Petrocelli singled to center, advancing Fisk to third and scoring Yastrzemski. Score: Red Sox 2, Reds 1. Evans walked, advancing Petrocelli to second. Pedro Borbon replaced Billingham as Reds pitcher. Burleson popped to center. 1 run, 2 hits, 3 left.

Reds ninth - Bench led off the inning with a double to right. Drago replaced Lee as Red Sox hurler. Perez was thrown out Burleson to Cooper, Bench advancing to third. Foster popped to left. Concepcion picked up an infield single, scoring Bench. Score: Red Sox 2, Reds 2. Concepcion stole second. Griffey doubled to center, scoring Concepcion. Score: Red Sox 2, Reds 3. Geronimo walked. Eastwick forced Geronimo, Doyle to Burleson. 2 runs, 3 hits, 2 left.

game 3

reds 6, red sox 5

BOSTON	ab	r	h	bi
Cooper, 1b	5	0	0	0
Doyle, 2b	5	0	1	0
Yastrzemski, lf	4	1	0	0
Fisk, c	3	1	1	1
Lynn, cf	3	0	1	1
Petrocelli, 3b	4	1	2	0
Evans, rf	4	1	2	2
Burleson, ss	4	0	2	0
Wise, p	2	0	0	0
Burton, p	0	0	0	0
Cleveland, p	0	0	0	0
Carbo, ph	1	1	1	1
Willoughby, p	0	0	0	0
Moret, p	0	0	0	0
Totals	35	5	10	5

CINCINNATI	ab	r	h	bi
Rose, 3b	4	1	1	0
Griffey, rf	3	0	0	0
Rettenmund, ph	1	0	0	0
Morgan, 2b	4	0	1	2
Perez, 1b	3	1	0	0
Bench, c	4	1	1	2
Foster, lf	3	0	0	0
Concepcion, ss	4	1	1	1
Geronimo, cf	4	2	2	1
Nolan, p	1	0	0	0
Darcy, p	1	0	0	0
C. Carroll, p	0	0	0	0
McEnaney, p	1	0	1	0
Eastwick, p	0	0	0	0
Armbrister, ph	1	0	0	0
Totals	34	6	7	6

one out when winning run scored

Boston		010 001 1020—5
Cincinnati		000 230 0001—6

E-Fisk 2. DP-Boston 1, Cincinnati 2. LOB-Boston 5, Cincinnati 5. 3B-Rose. HR-Fisk, Bench, Concepcion, Geronimo, Carbo, Evans. SB-Foster, Perez, Griffey. S-Willoughby. SF-Morgan, Lynn.

	ip	h	r	er	bb	so
Wise	4⅓	4	5	5	2	1
Burton	⅓	0	0	0	1	0
Cleveland	1⅓	0	0	0	0	2
Willoughby [L]	3	2	1	0	0	1
Moret	⅓	1	0	0	1	1
Nolan	4	3	1	1	1	0
Darcy	2	2	1	1	2	0
C. Carroll	⅔	1	1	1	0	0
McEnaney	1⅔	1	1	1	0	2
Eastwick [W]	1⅔	3	1	1	0	0

Darcy pitched to 1 batter in 7th; Willoughby pitched to 2 batters in 10th.
WP-Darcy
Time 3:03
Attendance 55,392

how the runs were scored

RED SOX second: Fisk homered to right field. Lynn popped to Geronimo. Petrocelli singled to left. Evans popped to right. Burleson forced Petrocelli, Concepcion to Morgan. One run, two hits, one left. Boston leads, 1-0.

REDS fourth: Griffey popped to center. Morgan lined to center. Perez walked. Bench homered, scoring Perez. Foster grounded out, Petrocelli to Cooper. Two runs, one hit, no runners left. Reds lead, 2-1.

REDS fifth: Concepcion homered. Geronimo homered. Darcy struck out. Rose tripled to center. Griffey walked and stole second. Morgan hit a sacrifice fly, scoring Rose. Perez struck out. Three runs, three hits, one left. Reds lead, 5-1.

RED SOX sixth: Doyle popped to Rose. Yastrzemski walked. Fisked walked. Yastrzemski advanced to second. A wild pitch by Darcy advanced Yastrzemski to third, Fisk to second. Lynn hit a sacrifice fly, scoring Yastrzemski. Petrocelli grounded out, Concepcion to Perez. One run, no hits, one left. Reds lead, 5-2.

RED SOX seventh: Evans singled to center. Clay Carroll relieved Pat Darcy on the mound for the Reds. Burleson hit into a double play, Morgan to Concepcion to Perez. Carbo hit a home run. Will McEnaney releived Carroll. Cooper popped to Concepcion. One run, two hits, nobody left. Reds lead, 5-3.

RED SOX ninth: Lynn struck out. Petrocelli singled to center. Evans homered, scoring Petrocelli. Burleson singled to center. Willoughby sacrificed Burleson to second. Cooper popped to center. Two runs, three hits, one left. Score tied, Reds 5-Red Sox 5.

REDS tenth: Geronimo singled to center. Armbrister bunted. Geronimo to second. Fisk's throw to second went into centerfield, both runners advancing a base. Rose walked. Griffey struck out. Morgan singled to center, scoring Geronimo. Reds win, 6-5.

game 4

red sox 5, reds 4

BOSTON	ab	r	h	bi
Beniquez	4	0	1	1
R. Miller, lf	1	0	0	0
Doyle, 2b	5	0	1	0
Yastrzemski, 1b	4	0	2	1
Fisk, c	5	1	1	0
Lynn, cf	4	1	1	0
Petrocelli, 3b	4	0	1	0
Evans, rf	4	1	2	2
Burleson, ss	4	1	1	1
Tiant, p	3	1	1	0
Totals	34	4	9	4

CINCINNATI	ab	r	h	bi
Rose, 3b	3	1	1	0
Griffey, rf	5	0	1	1
Morgan, 2b	3	1	0	0
T. Perez, 1b	4	0	0	0
Bench, c	4	0	1	1
G. Foster, lf	4	1	2	0
Concepcion, ss	4	1	1	1
Geronimo, cf	4	0	3	1
Norman, p	1	0	0	0
Borbon, p	0	0	0	0
Crowley, ph	1	0	0	0
C. Carroll, p	0	0	0	0
Chaney, ph	1	0	0	0
Eastwick, p	0	0	0	0
Armbrister, ph	0	0	0	0
Totals	34	4	9	4

Boston	000	500	000-5
Cincinnati	200	200	000-4

E-T. Perez, Doyle. DP-Cincinnati 1. LOB-Bostom 8, Cincinnati 8. 2B-Griffey, Bench, Burleson, Concepcion. 3B-Evans, Geronimo. S-Armbrister.

	ip	h	r	er	bb	so
Tiant [W, 2-0]	9	9	4	4	4	4
Norman [L, 0-1]	3⅓	7	4	4	1	2
Borbon	⅔	2	1	0	0	0
C. Carroll	2	2	0	0	0	2
Eastwick	3	0	0	0	1	0

WP-Norman.
Time 2:52
Attendance 55,667

how the runs were scored

REDS first: Rose singled to center. Griffey doubled to left center and was out trying to stretch it to a triple, Lynn to Burleson to Petrocelli, with Rose scoring on the play. Morgan walked. Burleson threw out Perez. Bench doubled to center to drive in Morgan. Petrocelli threw out Foster. Two runs, three hits, one left. Reds lead, 2-0.

RED SOX fourth: Fisk singled to center. Lynn singled to right. Fisk going to second. Petrocelli popped to Concepcion. Both runners advanced on a wild pitch. Evans tripled to center, scoring Fisk and Lynn. Burleson doubled to left to drive in Evans. Borbon replaced Norman. Tiant singled to center, Burleson stopping at third. Perez fumbled Beniquez's grounder as Burleson scored and Tiant advanced to second. Credit Beniquez with an RBI. Doyle fouled to Rose. Yastrzemski singled to center to score Tiant and send Beniquez to third. Fisk flied to Geronimo. Five runs, six hits, two left. Red Sox lead, 5-2.

REDS fourth: Perez struck out. Bench flied to Beniquez. Foster singled to Doyle and advanced to second when Doyle's throw went into the dugout. Concepcion blooped a double to center to score Foster. Geronimo tripled to left, Concepcion scoring. Crowley, pinch hitting for Borbon, struck out. Two runs, three hits, one left. Red Sox win, 5-4.

game 5

reds 6, red sox 2

BOSTON	ab	r	h	bi
Beniquez, lf	3	0	0	0
Doyle, 2b	4	1	1	0
Yastrzemski, 1b	3	1	1	1
Fisk, c	4	0	1	0
Lynn, cf	4	0	1	1
Petrocelli, 3b	4	0	0	0
Evans, rf	3	0	1	0
Burleson, ss	3	0	0	0
Cleveland, p	2	0	0	0
Willoughby, p	0	0	0	0
Griffin, ph	1	0	0	0
Pole, p	0	0	0	0
Segui, p	0	0	0	0
Totals	31	2	5	2

CINCINNATI	ab	r	h	bi
Rose, 3b	3	0	2	1
Griffey, rf	4	0	1	0
Morgan, 2b	3	1	1	0
Bench, c	3	2	1	0
Perez, 1b	3	2	2	4
Foster, lf	4	0	0	0
Concepcion, ss	2	0	0	1
Geronimo, cf	4	0	0	0
Gullett, p	3	1	1	0
Eastwick, p	0	0	0	0
Totals	29	6	8	6

Boston	100	000	001-2
Cincinnati	000	113	01x-6

DP-Boston 2. LOB-Boston 4, Cincinnati 5.
2B-Rose, Lynn. 3B-Doyle. HR-Perez 2. SB-Morgan, Concepcion. SF-Yastrzemski, Concepcion.

	ip	h	r	er	bb	so
Cleveland [L]	5	7	5	5	2	3
Willoughby	2	1	0	0	0	1
Pole	0	0	1	1	2	0
Segui	1	0	0	0	0	0
Gullett [W]	8⅔	5	2	2	1	7
Eastwick	⅓	0	0	0	0	1

Cleveland pitched to 3 batters in 6th; Pole pitched to 2 batters in 8th. HBP-by Willoughby [Concepcion].
Time 2:23
Attendance 56,393

how the runs were scored

RED SOX first: Beniquez grounded out, Morgan to Perez. Doyle tripled to right. Yastrzemski hit a sacrifice fly to right, scoring Doyle. Fisk struck out. One run, one hit, no runners left. Red Sox lead, 1-0.

REDS fourth: Morgan popped to right. Bench lined out to third. Perez homered. Foster popped to first. One run, one hit, no runners left.

REDS fifth: Concepcion grounded out, Petrocelli to Yastrzemski. Geronimo grounded out, Doyle to Yastrzemski. Gullett singled to center. Rose doubled to left, scoring Gullett. Griffey popped to third. One run, two hits, one left. Reds lead, 2-1.

REDS sixth: Morgan walked. Bench singled to right, Morgan going to third, Bench going to second on the throw to third. Perez homered, scoring Morgan and Bench. Willoughby replaced Cleveland. Foster lined out to right. Concepcion was hit by a pitch, stole second and moved to third on Geronimo's ground out to Yastrzemski. Gullett struck out. Three runs, two hits, one left. Reds lead, 5-1.

REDS eighth: Bench walked. Perez walked, advancing Bench to second. Foster flied to right. Concepcion hit a sacrifice fly, scoring Bench. Geronimo flied to center. One run, no hits, one left. Reds lead, 6-1.

RED SOX ninth: Beniquez struck out. Doyle grounded out,

Morgan to Perez. Yastrzemski singled. Fisk singled. Yastrzemski advancing to second. Lynn doubled to right, scoring Yastrzemski, Fisk advancing to third. Eastwick replaced Gullett. Petrocelli struck out. One run, three hits, two left. Reds win, 6-2.

game 6

red sox 7, reds 6

CINCINNATI	ab	r	h	bi		BOSTON	ab	r	h	bi
Rose, 3b	5	1	2	0		Cooper, 1b	5	0	0	0
Griffey, rf	5	2	2	2		Drago, p	0	0	0	0
Morgan, 2b	6	1	1	0		Miller, ph	1	0	0	0
Bench, c	6	0	1	1		Wise, p	0	0	0	0
Perez, 1b	6	0	2	0		Doyle, 2b	5	0	1	0
Foster, lf	6	0	2	2		Yastrzemski, 1b	6	1	3	0
Concepcion, ss	6	0	1	0		Fisk, c	4	2	2	1
Geronimo, cf	6	1	2	1		Lynn, cf	4	2	2	3
Nolan, p	1	0	0	0		Petrocelli, 3b	4	1	0	0
Chaney, ph	0	0	0	0		Evans, rf	5	0	1	0
Norman, p	0	0	0	0		Burleson, ss	3	0	0	0
Billingham, p	0	0	0	0		Tiant, p	2	0	0	0
Armbrister, ph	0	1	0	0		Moret, p	0	0	0	0
Carroll, p	0	0	0	0		Carbo, lf	2	1	1	3
Crowley, ph	1	0	1	0		Totals	41	7	10	7
Borbon, p	1	0	0	0						
Eastwick, p	0	0	0	0						
McEnaney, p	0	0	0	0						
Driessen, ph	1	0	0	0						
Darcy, p	0	0	0	0						
Totals	50	6	14	6						

none out when winning run scored

Cincinnati	000 030 210	000-6	
Boston	300 000 030	001-7	

E-Burleson. DP-Cincinnati 1, Boston 1. LOB-Cincinnati 11, Boston 9. 2B-Doyle, Evans, Foster. 3B-Griffey. HR-Lynn, Geronimo, Carbo, Fisk. SB-Concepcion. S-Tiant.

	ip	h	r	er	bb	so
Nolan	2	3	3	3	0	2
Norman	2/3	1	0	0	2	0
Billingham	1 1/3	1	0	0	1	1
Carroll	1	1	0	0	0	0
Borbon	2	1	2	2	2	1
Eastwick	1	2	1	1	1	2
McEnaney	1	0	0	0	1	0
Darcy [L]	2	1	1	1	0	1
Tiant	7	11	6	6	2	5
Moret	1	0	0	0	0	0
Drago	3	1	0	0	0	1
Wise, [W]	1	2	0	0	0	1

Tiant pitched to 1 batter in 8th; Borbon pitched to 2 batters in 8th; Eastwick pitched to 2 batters in 9th; Darcy pitched to 1 batter in 12th.

HBP-by Drago [Rose].

Time 4:01

Attendance 35,205

play by play

*indicates innings in which runs were scored

First inning:

CINCINNATI - Rose lined to Yastrzemski [slide catch]. Griffey walked. Morgan fouled to Fisk. Bench struck out. 0 runs, 0 hits, 0 errors, 1 man left on base.

* BOSTON- Cooper flied to Geronimo. Doyle grounded out Perez to Nolan. Yastrzemski singled to right. Fisk singled to left. Yaz holding second. Lynn homered to right. Petrocelli lined to Geronimo in deep left center. 3/3/0/0. Boston leads 3-0.

Second inning:

CINCINNATI- Perez struck out. Foster fouled to Cooper. Concepcion flied to Lynn. 0/0/0/0.

BOSTON - Evans was called out on strikes. Burleson grounded to Perez. Tiant was called out on strikes. 0/0/0/0. Boston leads 3-0.

Third inning:

CINCINNATI- Geronimo struck out. Chaney batted for Nolan and flied to Yastrzemski at the wall. Rose singled to center. Griffey grounded out Tiant to Doyle to Cooper. 0/1/0/1.

BOSTON- [Norman came in at pitcher.] Cooper popped to Concepcion in left. Doyle doubled to right down the line. Yastrzemski popped to Morgan. Fisk walked intentionally. Lynn walked. [Billingham replaced Norman at pitcher.] Petrocelli struck out. 0/1/0/3. Boston leads 3-0.

Fourth inning:

CINCINNATI-Morgan grounded hard to Doyle. Bench was called out on strikes. Perez singled to right. Burleson threw away Foster's grounder toward second, with Perez taking third. Concepcion fouled to Cooper. 0/1/2.

BOSTON- Evans hit a ground-rule double to right down the line. Burleson walked. Tiant sacrificed and was out Perez to Morgan. Cooper grounded to Perez. Doyle grounded to Morgan. 0/1/0/2. Boston leads 3-0.

Fifth inning:

* CINCINNATI-Geronimo lined to Evans. Armbrister batted for Billingham and walked. Rose singled to center, sending Armbrister to third. Griffey tripled off the left-center wall near the 379 sign [2 RBI]. Perez struck out. 3/3/0/1.

BOSTON- [Carroll came in at pitcher.] Yastrzemski singled to left. Fisk forced Yaz at second, Rose to Morgan. Lynn flied to Foster. Petrocelli forced Fisk at second, Concepcion to Morgan. 0/1/0/1. Score tied 3-3.

Sixth inning:

CINCINNATI-Foster grounded to Tiant right of the mound. Concepcion flied to Evans. Geronimo singled to left down the line. Crowley batted for Carroll and got a single when Burleson held his grounder. Rose grounded hard at Burleson, who stepped on second to force Crowley. 0/2/0/2.

BOSTON - [Borbon came in at pitcher.] Evans grounded hard to Morgan. Burleson walked. Tiant struck [foul bunt strike 3] out. Cooper grounded to Morgan. 0/0/0/1. Score tied 3-3.

Seventh inning:

* CINCINNATI- Griffey singled to right. Morgan singled to left, Griffey holding second. Bench flied to Yastrzemski on the track. Perez flied to Evans, Griffey taking third. Foster doubled off the center-field wall, scoring both

runners. Concepcion grounded to Burleson. 2/3/0/1.
Boston - Doyle popped to Concepcion. Yastrzemski grounded to Morgan. Fisk grounded to Concepcion. 0/0/0/0. Cincinnati leads 5-3.

Eighth inning
* CINCINNATI- Geronimo homered down the right-field line. [Moret replaced Tiant at pitcher.] Borbon grounded to Cooper. Rose grounded to Moret. Griffey flied to Lynn. 1/1/0/0.
* BOSTON- Lynn singled off Borbon's leg Petrocelli walked. [Eastwick replaced Borbon at pitcher.] Evans struck out. Burleson flied to Foster. Carbo batted for Moret and homered to center [3 RBI]. Cooper struck out. 3/2/0/0. Score tied 6-6.

Ninth inning:
Cincinnati- [Carbo stayed in the game in left field; Yastrzemski moved to first base; Drago came in at pitcher, batting in Cooper's spot.] Morgan popped to Yastrzemski. Bench grounded to Petrocelli. Perez fouled to Yastrzemski. 0/0/0/0.
BOSTON- Doyle walked. Yastrzemski singled to right, sending Doyle to third [McEnaney replaced Eastwick at pitcher.] Fisk walked intentionally. Lynn flied to Foster, who threw out Doyle at the plate for a double play; Yaz took third. Petrocelli grounded to Rose. 0/1/0/2. Score tied 6-6.

Tenth inning:
CINCINNATI- Foster grounded hard to Burleson. Concepcion singled to center. Concepcion stole second. Geronimo struck out. Driessen batted for McEnaney and popped to Carbo. 0/1/0/1.
BOSTON- [Darcy came in at pitcher.] Evans grounded to Darcy. Burleson popped to Concepcion. Carbo struck out. 0/0/0/0. Score tied 6-6.

Eleventh inning:
CINCINNATI-Rose was hit by a pitch [disputed call]. Griffey bunted and forced Rose at second Fisk to Burleson on a fine play. Morgan lined very deep to Evans who made a leaping catch and doubled Griffey off first, Evans to Yastrzemski to Burleson. 0/0/0/0.
BOSTON- Miller batted for Drago and flied to Foster. Doyle grounded to Concepcion. Yastrzemski grounded to Concepcion. 0/0/0/0. Score tied 6-6.

Twelfth inning:
CINCINNATI- Wise came in at pitcher. Bench fouled to Fisk. Perez singled to center. Foster singled to left. Concepcion flied to Evans. Geronimo was called out on strikes. 0/2/0/2.
BOSTON- Fisk homered onto the foul-pole screen in left. 1/1/0/0. Boston wins 7-6 in 12 innings.

Cincinnati	6	14	0	LP-Darcy
Boston	7	10	1	WP-Wise

game 7

reds 4, red sox 3

CINCINNATI	ab	r	h	bi		BOSTON	ab	r	h	bi
Rose, 3b	4	0	2	1		Carbo, lf	3	1	1	0
Morgan, 2b	4	0	2	1		Miller. lf	0	0	0	0
Bench, c	4	1	0	0		Beniquez, ph	1	0	0	0
Perez, 1b	5	1	1	2		Doyle, 2b	4	1	1	0
Foster, lf	4	0	1	0		Montgomery, ph	1	0	0	0
Concepcion, ss	4	0	1	0		Yastrzemski, 1b	5	1	1	1
Griffey, rf	2	2	1	0		Fisk, c	3	0	0	0
Geronimo, cf	3	0	0	0		Lynn, cf	2	0	0	0
Gullett, p	1	0	1	0		Petrocelli, 3b	3	0	1	1
Rettenmund, ph	1	0	0	0		Evans, rf	2	0	1	1
Billingham, p	0	0	0	0		Burleson, ss	3	0	0	0
Armbrister, ph	0	0	0			Lee, p	3	0	1	0
C. Carroll, p	0	0	0	0		Moret, p	0	0	0	0
Driessen, ph	1	0	0	0		Willoughby, p	0	0	0	0
McEnaney, p	0	0	0	0		Cooper, ph	1	0	0	0
Totals	33	4	9	4		Burton, p	0	0	0	0
						Cleveland, p	0	0	0	0
						Totals	31	3	5	3

```
Cincinnati        000   002   101-4
Boston            003   000   000-3
```
E-Doyle 2. DP-Cincinnati 1, Boston 2. LOB-Cincinnati 9, Boston 9. 2B-Carbo. HR-Perez. SB-Morgan, Griffey. S-Geronimo.

	ip	h	f	er	bb	so
Gullett	4	4	3	3	5	5
Billingham	2	1	0	0	2	1
C. Carroll [W]	2	0	0	0	1	1
McEnaney	1	0	0	0	0	0
Lee	1 1/3	7	3	3	1	2
Moret	1/3	1	0	0	2	0
Willoughby	1 1/3	0	0	0	0	0
Burton [L]	2/3	1	1	1	2	0
Cleveland	1/3	0	0	0	1	0

Save-McEnaney
WP-Gullett
Time 2:52
Attendance 35,205

play by play

*indicates innings in which runs were scored

First inning:
CINCINNATI- Rose popped to Evans. Morgan struck out. Bench grounded to Burleson. 0 runs, 0 hits, 0 errors, 0 men left on base.

BOSTON-Carbo doubled off the Wall in left center. Doyle flied to Griffey. Yastrzemski grounded to Morgan, Carbo taking third. Fisk struck out. 0/1/0/1. Score tied 0-0.

Second inning:
CINCINNATI - Perez grounded to Petrocelli. Foster singled off the Wall [scoreboard] but was out at second Carbo to Doyle. Concepcion grounded to Burleson [but

150

Yaz had to make a tag]. 0/1/0/0.

BOSTON- Lynn walked [Petrocelli hit a foul homer to left.] Petrocelli struck out. Evans fouled to Rose. Burleson flied to Griffey. 0/0/0/1. Score tied 0-0.

Third inning:
* CINCINNATI- Griffey singled to center. Geronimo grounded into a double play, Doyle to Burleson to Yastrzemski. Gullett singled to right. Rose grounded a ball hard off Lee's leg; it bounced to his right; he retrieved it and threw to Doyle to force Gullett. 0/2/0/1.

BOSTON- Lee struck out [foul bunt strike 3]. Carbo walked. Doyle singled to right, sending Carbo to third. Yastrzemski singled to right [RBI]; Doyle went to third and Yaz took second on the throw to third. Fisk walked intentionally. Lynn was called out on strikes. Petrocelli walked on 3-2 [RBI]. Evans walked on four pitches [RBI]. Burleson struck out. 3/2/0/3. Boston leads 3-0.

Fouth inning:
CINCINNATI- Morgan got a drag-bunt single. Bench flied to Lynn in the deep right-center corner [running catch]. Morgan stole second. Perez popped to Evans. Foster fouled to Fisk. 0/1/0/1. Boston leads 3-0.

BOSTON- Lee singled to right, then went to second on a wild pitch. Carbo grounded to Morgan behind second, sending Lee to third. Doyle grounded to Rose on a checked swing. Yastrzemski fouled to Morgan. 0/1/0/1. Boston leads 3-0.

Fifth inning:
CINCINNATI- Concepcion beat out a grounder to the first baseman for a hit. Griffey was safe on Doyle's error and Concepcion took third. Geronimo was called out on strikes. Rettenmund batted for Gullet and grounded into a double play, Burleson to Doyle to Yastrzemski. 0/1/1/1.

BOSTON-[Billingham came in at pitcher.] Fisk struck out. Lynn walked. Petrocelli singled to left, Lynn holding second. Evans flied very deep to Geronimo in center, Lynn advancing to third. Burleson walked. Lee flied deep to Geronimo. 0/1/3. Boston leads 3-0.

Sixth inning:
* CINCINNATI-Rose singled to right. Morgan flied to Evans. Bench forced Rose at second, Burleson to Doyle, but Doyle threw the ball in the dugout and Bench took second. Perez homered over the screen in left [2 RBI]. Foster flied to Evans. 2/2/1/0. Both runs earned.

BOSTON- Carbo grounded to Perez [the ball hit first base]. Doyle flied to Foster. Yastrzemski grounded to Morgan. 0/0/0/0. Boston leads 3-2.

Seventh inning:
* CINCINNATI- [Miller replaced Carbo in left.] Concepcion grounded to Burleson. Griffey walked. [Moret replaced Lee at pitcher.] Geronimo popped to Burleson. Armbrister batted for Billingham. Griffey stole second. Armbrister walked. Rose singled to center, scoring Griffey and sending Armbrister to third; Rose took second on the throw to the plate. Morgan walked. [Willoughby replaced Moret at pitcher.] Bench fouled to Fisk. 1/1/0/3. Run charged to Lee.

BOSTON - [Carroll came in at pitcher.] Fisk struck out. Lynn grounded out Perez to Carroll. Petrocelli grounded to Concepcion. 0/0/0/0. Score tied 3-3.

Eighth inning:
CINCINNATI- Perez popped to Petrocelli. Foster grounded to Burleson. Concepcion grounded to Petrocelli. 0/0/0/0.

BOSTON -Evans walked. Burleson grounded into a double play, Rose to Morgan to Perez. Cooper batted for Willoughby and fouled to Rose 0/0/0/0. Tied 3-3.

Ninth inning:
* CINCINNATI-[Burton came in at pitcher.] Griffey walked. Geronimo sacrificed and Petrocelli, sitting down, threw him out to Doyle. Driessen batted for Carroll and grounded to Doyle [Griffey to third]. Rose walked, Morgan singled to center, scoring Griffey, sending Rose to third and going to second on the throw to third. [Cleveland replaced Burton at pitcher]. Bench walked. Perez flied to Evans 1/1/0/3.

BOSTON- McEnaney came in at pitcher. Beniquez batted for Miller and lined to Griffey. Montgomery batted for Doyle and grounded hard to Concepcion. Yastrzemski flied to Geronimo 0/0/0/0.

Cincinnati	4	9	0	WP-Carroll	SV-McEnaney
Boston	3	5	2	LP-Burton	

151

1975 cincinnati reds roster

Manager—Sparky Anderson (10)

Coaches—Alex Grammas (2), Ted Kluszewski (18), George Scherger (3),

No.		B	T	Hgt.	Wgt.	Born	Birthplace	Residence
	PITCHERS							
43	Billingham, Jack	R	R	6:04	215	2/21/43	Orlando, Fla.	Cincinnati, O.
34	Borbon, Pedro	R	R	6:02	185	12/ 2/46	Valverde, D.R.	Valverde, D.R.
36	Carroll, Clay	R	R	6:01	205	5/ 2/41	Clanton, Ala.	Bradenton, Fla.
44	Darcy, Pat	L	R	6:03	175	5/12/50	Troy, O.	Tucson, Ariz.
49	Eastwick, Rawly	R	R	6:03	180	10/24/50	Camden, N. J.	Haddonfield, N. J.
35	Gullett, Don	R	L	6:00	185	1/ 5/51	Lynn, Ky.	Lynn, Ky.
31	Kirby, Clay	R	R	6:03	195	6/25/48	Washington, D. C.	Alpine, Calif.
37	McEnaney, Will	L	L	6:00	180	2/14/52	Springfield, O.	Springfield, O.
38	Nolan, Gary	R	R	6:03	202	5/27/48	Herlong, Calif.	Cincinnati, O.
32	Norman, Fred	S	L	5:08	170	8/20/42	San Antonio, Tex.	Cincinnati, O.
	CATCHERS							
5	Bench, Johnny	R	R	6:01	205	12/ 7/47	Binger, Okla.	Cincinnati, O.
9	Plummer, Bill	R	R	6:01	200	3/21/47	Oakland, Calif.	Anderson, Calif.
	INFIELDERS							
12	Chaney, Darrel	L	R	6:01	180	3/ 9/48	Hammond, Ind.	Cincinnati, O.
13	Concepcion, Dave	R	R	6:02	170	6/17/48	Aragua, Venezuela	Maracay, Venezuela
17	Crowley, Terry	L	L	6:00	170	2/16/47	Staten Island, N. Y.	Baltimore, Md.
22	Driessen, Dan	L	R	5:11	187	7/29/51	Hilton Head, S. C.	Hilton Head, S. C.
23	Flynn, Doug	R	R	5:11	160	4/18/51	Lexington, Ky.	Lexington, Ky.
8	Morgan, Joe	L	R	5:07	155	9/19/43	Bonham, Tex.	Oakland, Calif.
24	Perez, Tony	R	R	6:02	215	5/14/42	Camaguey, Cuba	Santurce, P.R.
14	Rose, Pete	S	R	5:11	200	4/14/41	Cincinnati, O.	Cincinnati, O.
	OUTFIELDERS							
33	Armbrister, Ed	R	R	5:11	160	7/ 4/48	Nassau, Bahamas	Nassau, Bahamas
15	Foster, George	R	R	6:01	195	12/ 1/48	Tuscaloosa, Ala.	Hawthorne, Calif.
20	Geronimo, Cesar	L	L	6:02	175	3/11/48	El Seibo, D.R.	El Seibo, D.R.
30	Griffey, Ken	L	L	5:11	190	4/10/50	Donora, Pa.	Cincinnati, O.
26	Rettenmund, Merv	R	R	5:10	195	6/ 6/43	Flint, Mich.	Cincinnati, O.

Trainer—Larry Starr   Equipment Manager—Bernie Stowe
Traveling Secretary—Paul Campbell
Team Physician—Dr. George Ballou

1975 statistics-cincinnati reds

BATTING	Pct.	G	AB	R	H	TB	2B	3B	HR	RBI	SH-SF	BB	SO	HB	SB-CS
Armbrister	.185	59	65	9	12	13	1	0	0	2	1-0	5	19	1	3-1
Bench	.283	142	530	83	150	275	39	1	28	110	0-8	65	108	2	11-0
Chaney	.219	71	160	18	35	47	6	0	2	26	0-1	14	38	0	3-0
Concepcion	.274	140	507	62	139	179	23	1	5	49	6-4	39	51	2	33-6
Crowley	.268	66	71	8	19	28	6	0	1	11	0-0	7	6	0	0-0
Driessen	.281	88	210	38	59	90	8	1	7	38	0-2	35	30	2	10-3
Flynn	.268	88	127	17	34	44	7	0	1	20	4-1	11	13	0	3-0
Foster	.300	134	463	71	139	240	24	4	23	78	0-5	40	73	3	2-1
Geronimo	.257	148	501	69	129	182	25	5	6	53	3-1	48	97	4	13-5
Griffey	.305	132	463	95	141	186	15	9	4	46	6-3	67	67	1	16-7
Morgan	.327	146	498	107	163	253	27	6	17	94	0-6	132	52	3	68-10
Perez	.282	137	511	74	144	238	28	3	20	109	0-6	54	101	3	1-2
Plummer	.182	65	159	17	29	39	7	0	1	19	0-4	24	28	2	1-0
Rettenmond	.239	93	188	24	45	59	6	1	2	19	1-2	35	22	0	5-0
Rose	.317	162	662	112	210	286	47	4	7	74	1-1	89	50	11	0-1
Team Totals	.271	162	5581	840	1515	2239	278	37	124	779	66-45	691	916	35	169-36

PITCHING	W	L	ERA	G	GS	CG	GF	SV	SHO	IP	H	HR	R	ER	BB	SO	HB
Billingham	15	10	4.11	33	32	5	0	0	0	208	222	22	100	95	76	79	9
Borbon	9	5	2.95	67	0	0	24	5	0	125	145	6	47	41	21	29	3
Carroll	7	5	2.63	56	2	0	27	7	0	96	93	2	30	28	32	44	3
Darcy	11	5	3.57	27	22	1	3	1	0	131	134	4	54	52	59	46	0
Eastwick	5	3	2.60	58	0	0	41	22	0	90	77	6	26	26	25	61	2
Gullett	15	4	2.42	22	22	8	0	0	3	160	127	11	49	43	56	98	2
Kirby	10	6	4.70	26	19	1	3	0	0	111	113	13	63	58	54	48	5
McEnaney	5	2	2.47	70	0	0	38	15	0	91	92	6	29	25	23	48	2
Nolan	15	9	3.16	32	32	5	0	0	1	211	202	18	75	74	29	74	1
Norman	12	4	3.73	34	26	2	1	0	0	188	163	23	85	78	84	119	0
Team Totals	108	54	3.37	162	162	22	140	50	8	1459	1422	112	586	546	487	663	29

1975 boston red sox roster

Manager—Darrell Johnson (22)

Coaches—Don Bryant (31), John Pesky (35),
Eddie Popowski (54), Stan Williams (32), Don Zimmer (34)

No.		B	T	Hgt.	Wgt.	Born	Birthplace	Residence
	PITCHERS							
43	Burton, Jim	R	L	6:03	195	10/27/49	Royal Oak, Mich.	Rochester, Mich.
26	Cleveland, Reggie	R	R	6:01	195	5/23/48	Swift Current, Sask.	St. Petersburg, Fla.
41	Drago, Dick	R	R	6:01	190	6/25/45	Toledo, O.	Overland Park, Kan.
37	Lee, Bill	L	L	6:03	210	12/28/46	Burbank, Calif.	Stoughton, Mass.
29	Moret, Rogelio	S	L	6:04	175	9/16/49	Guayama, P.R.	Guayama, P.R.
45	Pole, Dick	R	R	6:03	210	10/13/50	Trout Creek, Mich.	Trout Creek, Mich.
28	Segui, Diego	R	R	6:00	180	8/17/38	Holquin, Cuba	Kansas City, Kan.
23	Tiant, Luis	R	R	5:11	190	11/23/40	Havana, Cuba,	Milton, Mass.
38	Willoughby, Jim	R	R	6:02	185	1/31/49	Salinas, Calif.	Gustine, Calif.
40	Wise, Rick	R	R	6:02	195	9/13/45	Jackson, Mich.	Chesterfield, Mo.
	CATCHERS							
39	Blackwell, Tim	S	R	5:11	180	8/19/52	San Diego, Calif.	San Diego, Calif.
27	Fisk, Carlton	R	R	6:02	210	12/26/47	Bellows Falls, Vt.	Raymond, N. H.
10	Montgomery, Bob	R	R	6:01	203	4/16/44	Nashville, Tenn.	Dedham, Mass.
	INFIELDERS							
7	Burleson, Rick	R	R	5:10	165	4/29/51	Lynwood, Calif.	Acton, Mass.
17	Cooper, Cecil	L	L	6:02	185	12/20/49	Brenham, Tex.	Brenham, Tex.
5	Doyle, Denny	L	R	5:10	165	1/17/44	Glasgow, Ky.	Laurel Springs, N. J.
2	Griffin, Doug	R	R	6:00	160	6/ 4/47	South Gate, Calif.	Peabody, Mass.
12	Heise, Bob	R	R	5:11	170	5/12/47	San Antonio, Tex.	Vacaville, Calif.
6	Petrocelli, Rico	R	R	6:00	190	6/27/43	Brooklyn, N. Y.	Lynnfield, Mass
8	Yastrzemski, Carl	L	R	5:11	190	8/22/39	Southampton, N. Y.	Boston, Mass.
	OUTFIELDERS							
20	Beniquez, Juan	R	R	5:11	165	5/13/50	San Sebastian, P.R.	San Sebastian, P.R.
1	Carbo, Bernie	L	R	6:00	175	8/ 5/47	Detroit, Mich.	Allen Park, Mich.
24	Evans, Dwight	R	R	6:03	205	11/ 3/51	Santa Monica, Calif.	Reading, Mass.
19	Lynn, Fred	L	L	6:01	185	2/ 3/52	Chicago, Ill.	El Monte, Calif.
16	Miller, Rick	L	L	6:00	180	4/19/48	Grand Rapids, Mich.	Boston, Mass.
*14	Rice, Jim	R	R	6:02	200	3/ 8/53	Anderson, S. C.	Anderson, S. C.

*On disabled list

Trainer—Charles Moss   Equipment Manager—Pete Cerrone
Traveling Secretary—Jack Rogers
Team Physician—Dr. Thomas Tierney

1975 statistics-boston red sox

BATTING	Pct.	G	AB	R	H	TB	2B	3B	HR	RBI	SH-SF	BB	SO	HB	SB-CS
Beniquez	.291	78	254	43	74	102	14	4	2	17	6-1	25	26	2	7-10
Blackwell	.197	59	132	15	26	33	3	2	0	6	5-0	19	13	1	0-0
Burleson	.252	158	580	66	146	191	25	1	6	62	17-9	45	44	3	8-5
Carbo	.257	107	319	64	82	154	21	3	15	50	1-3	83	69	1	2-4
Cooper	.311	106	305	49	95	166	17	6	14	44	3-3	19	33	3	1-4
Doyle	.298	97	325	50	97	134	21	2	4	36	10-2	15	12	1	5-7
Evans	.274	128	412	61	113	188	24	6	13	56	5-2	47	60	4	3-4
Fisk	.331	79	263	47	87	139	14	4	10	52	0-2	27	32	2	4-3
Griffin	.240	100	287	21	69	78	6	0	1	29	7-2	18	29	2	2-2
Heise	.214	63	126	12	27	30	3	0	0	21	4-2	4	6	2	0-0
Lynn	.331	145	528	103	175	299	47	7	21	105	6-6	62	90	3	10-5
Miller	.194	77	108	21	21	25	2	1	0	15	2-0	21	20	0	3-2
Montgomery	.226	62	195	16	44	62	10	1	2	26	3-3	4	37	1	1-1
Petrocelli	.239	115	402	31	96	134	15	1	7	59	3-5	41	66	3	0-2
Rice	.309	144	564	92	174	277	29	4	22	102	1-8	36	122	4	10-5
Yastrzemski	.269	149	543	91	146	220	30	1	14	60	0-2	87	67	2	8-4
Team Totals	.275		5448	798	1500	2274	284	44	134	756	75-53	565	741	34	66-58

PITCHING	W	L	ERA	G	GS	CG	SV	SHO	IP	H	HR	R	ER	BB	SO	HB
Burton	1	2	2.89	29	4	0	1	0	53.0	58	6	30	17	19	39	0
Cleveland	13	9	4.43	31	20	3	0	1	170.2	173	19	90	84	52	98	3
Drago	2	2	3.84	40	2	0	15	0	72.2	69	5	31	31	31	43	0
Lee	17	9	3.95	41	34	17	0	0	260.0	274	20	123	114	69	78	3
Moret	14	3	3.60	36	16	4	1	1	145.0	132	8	60	58	76	80	2
Pole	4	6	4.42	18	11	2	0	1	89.2	102	11	46	44	32	42	2
Segui	2	5	4.82	33	1	1	6	0	71.0	71	10	41	38	43	45	0
Tiant	18	14	4.02	35	35	18	0	2	260.0	262	25	126	116	72	142	4
Willoughby	5	2	3.54	24	0	0	8	0	48.1	46	6	25	19	16	29	2
Wise	19	12	3.95	35	35	17	0	1	255.1	262	34	126	112	72	141	4
Team Totals	95	65	3.98	327	160	62	31	10	1436.2	1463	145	709	636	490	720	20

153

PACKED HOUSE -- Cincinnati fans jammed the Fountain Square area of the Queen City to welcome home the '75 World Champs.

spring training

LETTING IT ALL HANG OUT-- The pitchers don special pants to practice base sliding (above) during spring workouts; Gary Nolan works with pitching coach Larry Shepard (left), a view of the Al Lopez Field (below); Will McEnaney goes into his slide.

season highlights

YOU WERE GREAT, JOE -- Morgan was a runaway winner in the National League's Most Valuable Player balloting.

THAT HIT BY PETE ROSE
WAS THE 2,500TH OF HIS
MAJOR LEAGUE CAREER
HE'S THE 52ND PLAYER
IN HISTORY TO REACH
THE 2,500 MARK

THE SCOREBOARD TELLS THE STORY -- Pete Rose bangs out his 2,500 hit at Riverfront (opposite); Clay Carroll breaks Joe Nuxhall's record for most appearances in a Reds' uniform.

SHOT DOWN BY BLANKS -- A line drive off the bat of Atlanta's Larvell Blanks broke the left thumb of hurler Don Gullett. The incident, which occurred on June 16, kept Gullett out of action for two months.

BRINGING 'EM HOME -- Tony Perez became the Reds all time RBI king in '75 when he knocked in his 1010th runner.

VICTORY SHOWERS -- Pat Darcy and Will McEnaney give themselves a shampoo after the Reds clinched their division title on September 7th.

I'M GETTING OUT OF HERE -- Johnny Bench has had enough celebrating for one day.

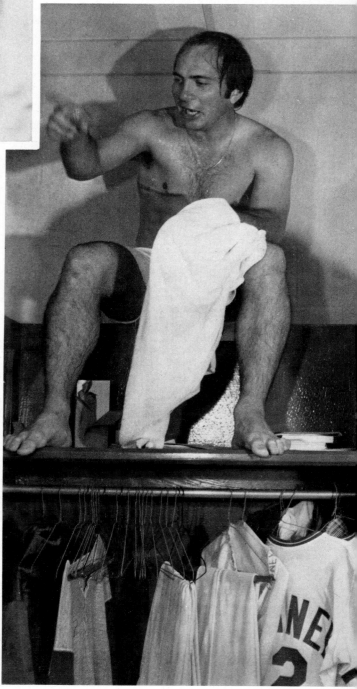

AIN'T IT SWEET

BEST IN THE WEST -- Will McEnaney douses Reds President Bob Howsam after the club had clinched the N. L. West.

SCOOPING UP THE GROUNDER--Don Gullett's diminutive son snags a sharp liner.

fathers

A ROSE BY ANY OTHER NAME-- Pete Rose's son displays that familiar Rose swing.

WHAT'S A BASEBALL, DAD? -- Clay Carroll's son seems a bit unsure of himself on the diamond.

ON THE BENCH -- The two Perez boys (left) join the two sons of Pedro Borbon on the young Reds bench.

and sons

GRIFFEY POWER -- Ken Griffey's son, who appears to be wearing his father's batting helmet, takes a big swing.

UNDER THE TAG -- Doug Flynn (left) and Merv Rettenmund watch as a speeding Perez slides under the tag to score a run for the sons.

husbands

KEEP MOVING -- Pete Rose gives his wife Karolyn a friendly pat to remind her to keep hustling.

THE GULLETT ZIP-- Cathy Gullett warms up her arm before she faces the dangerous Red Machine.

LOW BRIDGE-- Robin Plummer kicks up some dust as she slides in for another score for the wives club.

MEAN AND HUNGRY-- The wives club is awesome sight as they line up before the annual game with their husbands.

DO IT THIS WAY, HONEY -- Johnny Bench explains the importance of bat position to his wife, Vickie.

and wives

BIRD ON THE FLY -- Birdie Griffey wings one homeward.

MIGHTY CROWLEY HAS STRUCK OUT -- Terry Crowley's wife isn't the least bit happy with being called out on strikes.

all stars

THE BEST IN THE BUSINESS -- The two squads were introduced in a pre-game ceremony (above); Joe Morgan and Rod Carew chat before the game (below, right); Johnny Bench and Thurman Munson were voted the two best catchers in the game (below).

ALL STAR ACTION -- Pete Rose and Joe Morgan lead the cheering in the National League dugout (above); Dave Concepcion handles a tag play on Cleveland's George Hendrick (above, right); Pete Rose made a return to the outfield for the All Star game (below, right); Tony Perez zeroes in on a pitch (below).

FUN ON FARMERS NIGHT-- Johnny Bench goes after a full pail of milk; Dave Concepcion uses his soft touch in the egg throwing contest; George Scherger, who is wearing the blindfold, wheelbarrows his way towards home plate.

the playoffs

PLAYOFF STARTERS-- Gary Nolan, Don Gullett and Fred Norman started the Playoff games for the Reds.

I FINALLY GOT ONE -- Don Gullett proudly exhibits the bat he used to crack a home run in the first game of the Playoffs against the Pirates. It was Don's first major league round-tripper.

JUST DIDN'T HAVE IT TODAY -- Jerry Reuss lasted just 2.2 innings against the Reds in the opening game of the Playoffs. Reuss gave up 4 runs on 4 hits to Cincinnati.

GAME TWO HERO-- Tony Perez came through with 3 hits in 4 plate appearances to drive in 3 runs in game two of the Playoffs.

COULD YOU REPEAT THE QUESTION -- With Pirates Jerry Reuss and Danny Murtaugh watching, Sparky Anderson answers a question at a press conference during the Playoffs.

THE CHIEF IS AMBUSHED -- Cesar Geronimo, who is known as "The Chief," is tagged out at home by Pirate Catcher Manny Sanguillen.

TALENTED TRIO--Joe Morgan, Willie Stargell and Tony Perez got together before the Playoff opener.

STEALING THEM BLIND
--Joe Morgan's base stealing was a major factor in the Reds Playoff sweep of the Pirates. He stole six bases in the three game series.

COOL OFF, FRANK -- Pirate coach Bob Skinner pulls Frank Taveras away from a dispute with an umpire during the Championship Series.

WE'RE GONNA BEAT YA, DANNY -- Sparky Anderson seems to be giving a Playoff prediction to a rather skeptical Danny Murtaugh.

CHEERING THE CHAMPS ON -- Dick Wagner (left), Bob and Janet Howsam, and Louis Nippert lead the cheering for the Red Machine in the Playoffs.

PETE CHIPS IN-- Pete Rose added a game tying home run to the Reds cause in the third game of the Playoffs in Pittsburgh.

PLAYOFF SWEEP COMPLETED

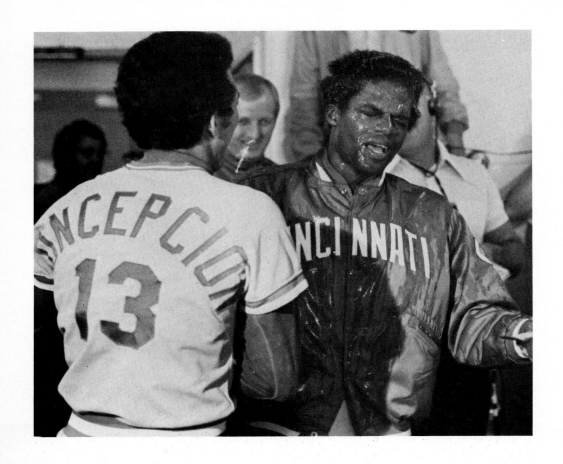

CLUBHOUSE

BEDLAM

IN

PITTSBURGH

the manager
and
the coaches

sparky anderson

At 41, Sparky Anderson has already established himself as one of baseball's all time great managers... his clubs have won an astounding total of 581 games in 6 years... it's been an amazing success story for a man who came to the Reds in 1970 as a complete unknown... he had managed for five years prior to taking over the Reds... Anderson's chief strength is his ability to keep his men in a competitive yet harmonious spirit... undeniably, he's worked with a lot of talent on the Reds, but many managers have had talented clubs... it takes that little extra from the man at the helm to motivate those gifted players to do their job... he runs a disciplined club, but the players don't feel he's rigid in his enforcement of the rules... the pitchers call him "Captain Hook" because he is often quick to pull them when they get into trouble... but with a bullpen like the one Anderson had in '75, it would be hard to find fault with his quick hook... he's a very likable man and is exceedingly patient with the demanding press... because of his involved baseball stories and his delightful personality, he's often compared to Casey Stengel... he's an elegant dresser who says "clothes are like a disease with me"...

alex grammas

    Alex "The Greek" Grammas came to Cincinnati in 1970, after having spent five years coaching with the Pittsburgh Pirates... ironically, he served as interim manager of the Bucs in '69, replacing the dismissed manager, Larry Shepard... played major league ball with the Reds, Cardinals and Cubs... was known for his prowess in the infield... is thought to be an excellent handler of men as well as one of the better tacticians in the big leagues... it came as no surprise that Alex decided to sign on as manager of the Milwaukee Brewers beginning in '76... several clubs have shown interest in him through the years... is a debonair fellow who has impeccable taste in clothing...

ted kluszewski

"Big Klu" is one of the most well respected batting coaches in baseball... has a very subtle approach, and will not force himself upon hitters... his specialty is picking up that minor defect in a player's swing that is causing problems... is a real student of hitting... will spend hours going over films of Reds hitters... some power hitters on the club will occasionally ask him to tap their bats during close games, hoping some of his "home run magic" will rub off... has a mild disposition and a fine sense of humor... is a good bridge player... was the first baseman on The Greatest Reds Ever team which was selected in '69... hit 279 career home runs and has a lifetime .298 batting average...

george scherger

It would be hard to find a coach in the majors who is more dedicated to his job than George Scherger... "Schugs" is a quiet fellow who works with incredible intensity... will spend hours on the diamond, hitting balls to players who want to sharpen their defense... has a complete knowledge of the fundamentals of the game... will no doubt prove successful in '76 when he replaces Alex Grammas as third base coach for the club... goes unrecognized by the press, but actually is one of the strongest "steadying" forces on the team... has a great ability for story telling... worked his way up through the minors, both as a player and coach...

larry shepard

Another hard working veteran on Sparky Anderson's coaching staff is Larry Shepard... "Shep" has the job of handling the Cincinnati pitching staff... is one of Anderson's closest advisors... cares deeply about his hurlers, both as athletes and as men... has played a key role in developing Don Gullett into one of the best pitchers in the game... like Ted Kluszewski, he spends much time watching films of his men... has been managing since 1948... served as skipper for the Pittsburgh Pirates for two seasons and also was the pitching coach for the Philadelphia Phils... enjoys playing bridge and chess for recreation... is very good at working crossword puzzles...

the players

ed armbrister

A few brief moments in the Championship Playoffs and the World Series saved the 1975 season for this Bahamian bench-warmer...Ed Armbrister, who came to the Reds along with Joe Morgan, Jack Billingham, Cesar Geronimo and Denis Menke in the celebrated '71 swap with Houston, had a nightmare of a regular season...''Bree'', as Armbrister is known to his teammates, played in 59 games, coming to bat only 65 times and hitting a miserable .185...he was used mainly as a pinch runner and fill-in outfielder...

But post-season play brought out the best in him... Ed's first moment of prominence came when, pinch hitting for the pitcher in the tenth inning, he lofted a perfect sacrifice fly that plated the winning run in the third and final game of the Playoffs with the Pittsburgh Pirates... oddly enough, Armbrister had only 2 RBI's during the entire regular season... ''It's the biggest thing that has happened to me this year,'' Ed said later. ''It was good that we completed the sweep. If a team like the Pirates would have won the game--well, once they get started winning, they don't know when to stop''...

Then in the third game of the World Series against the Boston Red Sox, Armbrister took part in a play that may place his name next to that of Fred Snodgrass in baseball folklore...the wire-drawn reserve, in the process of sacrificing the winning run to second in the bottom of the tenth inning, had a collision with Sox catcher Carlton Fisk in front of home plate--the mix up jarred Fisk enough to send his throw off the bag at second, allowing the lead runner to get to third and eventually come home on Joe Morgan's single... it was the kind of controversial incident that will haunt Armbrister the rest of his career...

As unbelievable as it may seem, Ed had only one sacrifice bunt in '75 before laying down that epic bunt in the Series...the 27-year old Armbrister is an easy going cut-up who loves music and dancing... a frequent sight in the Reds clubhouse several hours before game time was Ed lounging on the red-carpeted floor, entertaining some of his teammates with stories about his eight year minor league career...

Armbrister's goal for the future is to log more playing time...''I don't know what next year's plans are,'' he said near the end of the season. ''I just hope that I get a chance to play no matter where I'm at. Nobody can tell me I can't play good baseball if I get the chance''...

johnny bench

Sparky Anderson always chuckles when someone mentions that there is a new catcher in the minors "who looks like a young Johnny Bench"…Anderson points out that the "old" Johnny Bench is still pretty young himself…he turned 28 a month and a half after the Reds had beaten the Boston Red Sox in the 72nd World Series…Bench had a typically successful season in '75, even though he was handicapped most of the year by a shoulder injury…his .283 batting average was his highest since 1970 when he hit .293… he knocked in 110 RBI's, making '75 the fourth consecutive year that he's topped 100 in that department… he blasted 28 homers, the seventh consecutive time he's hit more than 25 in a season…

His physical problems began when he and Gary Matthews of the San Francisco Giants collided at home plate in a game at Riverfront Stadium on April 22nd…pain in his left shoulder stayed with him the rest of the year as a reminder of that collision…at times it forced him to change his batting stroke… it wasn't until after the season that Bench had corrective surgery…the operation to remove cartilage from the joint on top of his shoulder and a small section of bone from the collar bone was performed on November 17… by early December, Bench seemed fit as ever…

A late season foot injury compounded John's difficulties, probably keeping him from winning his fourth RBI crown…

Bench is a very worldly person who can handle himself well whether he's on national television or at the hospital bedside of an ailing child… makes frequent appearances at charity benefits… is a financially shrewd man who has made wise investments…

His "Home Plate" restaurant in Cincinnati is one of the best in town… goes out of his way for younger players on the team… he especially helped Doug Flynn and Don Werner learn the major league ropes… married Vickie Chesser in a Gatsby-like wedding ceremony in the Queen City shortly before spring training in '75…

He is a television game-show fan… is a very talented golfer… also enjoys hunting and tennis, although his time for recreation is limited… has a fine singing voice and may make show business a career when he retires from baseball… is called the "Little General" because of the forceful manner with which he directs traffic on the ball field…

jack billingham

This thirty two year old veteran righthander had a rugged season, but a couple of brilliant relief stints in the World Series salvaged things... Jack finished up with a 15-11 mark and a swollen ERA of 4.11... the 95 earned runs he gave up was the highest total on the Reds staff... Jack's best pitch, his curve ball, did not come around consistently at any time in the season...

Near the end of the year, at the suggestion of some of his teammates and his wife, "Cactus Jack" went to see a hypnotist... according to Billingham, the hypnotist believed that Jack was not throwing his curve correctly because, subconsciously, he was afraid of hurting his arm...

Nine sessions with the man apparently did the trick, as Billingham pitched very relaxed and very sharp ball against the Boston Red Sox...

Since joining the club in '71, Jack has put together some top flight marks... twice -- in '73 and '74 -- he won 19 games...

The '73 season was his best as a major leaguer... he didn't miss a start that year, led the league in shutouts with 7, tied with Steve Carlton of Philadelphia for most innings pitched [293] and had the third best complete game mark (16)...

The 32-year old Billingham tends to be somewhat of a deliberate pitcher, but the first thing he learned when he came to Cincinnati was to work fast on the mound... he no longer picks at the resin bag and takes his time - one of his keys to success is to get the ball back from the catcher and fire it right back in...

Because he is so easy going, many think he's not mean enough when he's pitching... that competitive fire is there, it's just hidden under a tranquil facade...

Off the field, one of Jack's main interests is fishing... he jokingly says that his son is looking forward to his retirement so that the two of them can get a boat and head for the fishing hole everyday... Billingham is very much of a family man, spending as much time at home in the off season as he can...

One baseball memory that Jack will carry with him the rest of his life came on Opening Day 1974 when the Reds met the Atlanta Braves... Hank Aaron smacked his 714th home run off Billingham in the first inning of that game... "Yep, I'll remember that one," Jack said later...

pedro borbon

Pedro Borbon has the distinction of having more nicknames than any other player on the Reds ballclub... ''Baboon'' and ''Boonie'' are two of the most common names Pedro is called, but some enthusiastic season ticket holders who sit by first base at Riverfront Stadium came up with a new sobriquet last season... because of Borbon's flamboyant manner on the mound, these fans refer to him as ''Jaunty''...

To no one's surprise, Pedro led the talented 1975 Cincinnati bullpen in innings pitched with 125... the colorful native of the Dominican Republic appeared in 67 games, the fourth straight year that he has appeared in more than 60 games... his 2.95 ERA was the second best ERA he has notched in his seven major league campaigns...

Borbon is noted for his durability... he often insists that he could pitch every day if the club wanted him to... he is also famous for his throwing stunts like trying to hit the top of the Astrodome with a ball or throwing a ball over home plate from deep centerfield...

Borbon is an awesome figure on the mound because opposing batters really aren't sure what he might pull next... he wears his ballcap cocked to one side and throws to the plate from all angles in what could be the best imitation of a Luis Tiant delivery in the majors...

In one of the few crucial games the Reds played early last season, Borbon was on the mound with two outs and men on first and second -- Manager Sparky Anderson, who is very aware of Pedro's idiosyncratic make-up, ran out on the mound and said, ''No tricks, Pedro. Let's just get the win''... with that firebrand spirit of his, all Pedro would have to do would be to put on a little more bulk and he'd be a fine professional hockey player...

In his early days as a pitcher, he was not known to have great control, but today he seldom is out of the strike zone... some of his pitches come toward the plate with an incredible amount of spin on them, dipping and darting around like fast knuckleballs... he once described one of his outings to an interviewer as a night when ''my ball, she move like a snake!''... would be the bullpen ace on the All Eccentric team...

clay carroll

Although used slightly less in '75 than he had been in previous years, this robust native of Clanton, Alabama, was still as effective as ever... "The Hawk" appeared in 56 games last season, a total which is six short of the 62 games he has averaged every year since joining the Reds in '68... Carroll still compiled a 7-5 record with a 2.63 ERA and had seven saves...

Clay is one of the few relievers in the history of baseball who has been able to sustain superior stats through 600 plus games... and at 34, he has superb command of all his pitches... "He still has the same stuff he always had," says Gary Waits, the Cincinnati bullpen catcher...

"I'm still 20 years old when I go to the mound," Carroll has said... one of the brightest moments he had in '75 came in late September when he passed Joe Nuxhall to become the all time Reds leader for appearances with 485...

Clay came to the Reds from Atlanta with Tony Cloninger and Woody Woodward in exchange for Milt Pappas, Ted Davidson and Bob Johnson... "I'm still holding up our end of the deal," the Hawk said kiddingly to television broadcaster Woodward last summer...

Clay is a friendly fellow who prides himself on his southern hospitality... "Back where I come from, they always speak to you first," he says... Carroll enjoys bringing his young son Bret into the Reds clubhouse after a few games during the regular season... although Bret is just a year old, he's already the spitting image of his dad... a few of his teammates kidded Clay last summer by telling him that Bret is slowly developing his father's almost loping gait...

Carroll's favorite recreation during the summer is working on a deep suntan... he averages around three hours a day lying out in the sun by the swimming pool at the Kentucky apartment house he lives in... during the off season, the Carroll family makes their home in Bradenton, Florida... that home in Bradenton is a beautiful ranch style residence which is dominated by a game-filled rumpus room...

Clay is a country and western music buff -- with his pleasant looks and folksy smile, the "Hawk" could almost pass as a bluegrass singing star himself...

tom carroll

Twenty three year old Tommy Carroll has yet to pitch a full season for the Reds, but all signs indicate that he'll have a brilliant major league career...for the last two years, Carroll has started off with the Cincinnati AAA club in Indianapolis and then has been summoned to the Reds in mid-season...in those two years, Tommy has totalled 12 wins against five losses... in '75, Carroll was promoted to the team when Don Gullett broke his thumb on June 16... "T. C." did the job that was asked of him, as he won four of five decisions...is a most sincere young man who has tremendous drive... has a herky-jerky delivery that is reminiscent of the way that Phil Regan used to pitch...

Carroll's head snaps skyward just as he comes through towards the plate... asked if he would ever switch to a more conventional motion, Tom says, "Heck no. It's more fun the way I do it"...

Right now the only thing that is really preventing him from having a full time spot in the majors is a slight control problem... Tom insists that if he was given a shot at being in a regular rotation for a season in the big leagues, he would prove equal to the task... many figure that '76 will be the year he gets that chance...

He has a refreshingly quick mind and is possibly the deepest thinker on the Reds club... is not afraid to tackle profound literature -- has actually been seen reading a book by Vladimir Nabokov in the Cincinnati clubhouse... very few of Tommy's teammates would even attempt to pronounce Vladimir Nabokov...

He attends Penn State University in the off season, as he's very conscious of the new life he'll have to make for himself when he gets out of baseball...

His idea of an enjoyable evening on the town is taking a date to an intimate restaurant which features international cuisine and having a long conversational meal... has singular taste in clothing: one day he'll show up in grubby bell bottoms and the next, he'll look like he just stepped out of a Brooks Brothers display case...

He roomed last season with fellow hurler Pat Darcy in an apartment in northern Kentucky... is not related to reliever Clay Carroll... plays a very aggressive game of tennis... also enjoys chess... likes to ski, but avoids it because he doesn't want to risk serious injury...

darrel chaney

Darrel Chaney's job with the Reds is not exactly the most envied position in all of baseball... as a utility infielder, the 27-year old Chaney sees much of his baseball while sitting on the Cincinnati bench... most of Darrel's playing opportunities come late in the game, when the score is close and a proven glove is required... that puts Chaney in the position of having to make the good play, despite the fact that he's been cooling on the sidelines and may not be completely loose...

Because he comes in at crucial times, his rather infrequent errors are well remembered by the fans... Darrell can play third, short and second, which makes him a valuable commodity...

Due to lack of playing time, Chaney has never been able to develop his hitting potential... his .219 batting average in '75 is the best mark he's had since he hit .250 in '72... the 26 RBI's he collected in '75 is a career high...

Oddly enough, when he was a younger player, Chaney was considered something of a power hitter... he clubbed 23 home runs and 21 doubles for Asheville in '68... Darrel's big season for the Reds came in '73 when he subbed for the injured Dave Concepcion at shortstop... Concepcion broke his left ankle just prior to the All Star game that year and Chaney had to fill his shoes for the remainder of the season...

His sparkling defense helped carry the club to the Championship Series... there has been much trade talk since the end of the '75 season, as many teams are showing interest in giving Darrel a full time job... in the winters of '73 and '74, he assisted Gordy Coleman in the Reds Speakers Bureau... in the offseason of '75, Darrel went to work at The Professionals, a Cincinnati-based agency which handles off-the-field engagements for many Queen City athletes... Chaney is a noted speaker, and someday plans to get into radio broadcasting... has appeared on several radio programs in the Ohio Valley area... was raised in Hammond, Indiana, where he was a high school football star... it was in high school that he picked up the tag, "Norton from Morton"... still called "Norton" by many of the Reds... has an excellent sense of humor and a real knack for telling a joke...

200

dave concepcion

Even though Dave Concepcion was handicapped by a broken bone in his right hand for two months of the season, he still turned in a remarkably consistent year... he was especially impressive in the field, where he is noted for his range at shortstop... the fleet Concepcion won his third consecutive Golden Glove for his defensive artistry..

He continued to develop his base-running skills during the year, as he swiped 33 bags and was caught only 6 times... in '74, Davey stole 41 bases in 47 attempts... he has good natural speed, and only needs improvement in the finer aspects of stealing...Joe Morgan continued to coach Concepcion during the season on the various things to watch for in a pitcher's delivery to get that extra little advantage... Dave is not the least bit afraid of being picked off: he easily takes the longest lead off first of any baserunner in the Senior Circuit...

In '75, he smacked 5 home runs and picked up 49 RBI... Davey connected for 14 homers and 82 RBI's in '74..

One of the biggest boosts that Concepcion has received in his major league career is the avid interest of Tony Perez... the two are roommates when the Reds go on the road, and Perez has spent much time working with the thin Venezuelan... the 27-year old Concepcion says that Tony has helped him to become less sensitive about his performance... Perez has taught him not to dwell on his bad days at the plate or in the field...

Davey's ultimate goal is to become the best Venezuelan shortstop in the history of baseball... his only rival for that title is the retired great, Luis Aparicio...

Dave's nickname is "Mague"...

Concepcion is on an almost steady diet of baseball, as he usually plays winter ball in Venezuela...

Outside of baseball, another of Davey's major interests in life is racing car driving... he's been known to run Volkswagens in racing competition during the off season...

His beautiful wife Delia gave birth to the Concepcion's first child during the '75 season... the latest addition to the family is named David Alexander Concepcion...

terry crowley

Terry Crowley, the 28-year old first baseman, plays defense for the Reds about as often as Pete Rose misses a game... but that's all right with the "Crow"...

He gets paid for his reliable bat, not his fielding... in '75, Crowley was Sparky Anderson's top pinch-hitter... in one streak in April and May, he reached base eight straight times in pinch hit roles...

He may not be the fastest man on the Reds roster, but he still collected 6 doubles during the year... his biggest asset as a pinch-hitter is an uncanny ability to make contact... Terry fanned only six times in 71 at bats in '75...

Crowley came to Cincinnati from the Texas Rangers in a cash deal just shortly before the '74 season... the left handed native of Staten Island, New York, was also the Reds best pinch hitter in '74...

Although he might not say so, he is something of a gourmet... Terry is very fond of sea food, especially fresh lobster...

One of his favorite dishes is a ravioli and Italian sausage combination plate which his wife Janet cooks to perfection... Terry met Janet when the two were just freshmen at Curtis High School in Staten Island, and they dated throughout their four years there...

While he was in high school, Terry was captain of his baseball team and also played basketball... he still has an avid interest in sports and will attend football, basketball and hockey games when he gets the chance...

The Crowleys reside in Baltimore during the winter months... his best friend on the team is Merv Rettenmund... the two former Orioles were roommates in Baltimore and now share a room when the Reds go on the road... Terry and Merv were invaluable during the World Series with Boston, as they were able to furnish tips on both Luis Tiant's pitching and the best way to play the field in the treacherous Fenway Park...

During the Series, Crowley got a chance to display his writing prowess... he wrote an occasional column for a newspaper in Staten Island...

Crowley is a soft spoken man who has a friendly word for everyone...

pat darcy

Pat Darcy, a hard throwing righthander, made an unexpected breakthrough into the big leagues in '75... very few in the Cincinnati spring camp tabbed Darcy as the Reds fourth starter, but his determination and hard work earned him the shot... he started 22 games for Cincinnati during the regular season, the fourth highest total among the starters on the team's staff... his strength on the mound is keeping the ball away from the opposition's power hitters... he gave up just four homers in 131 innings pitched... only Clay Carroll, who gave up two roundtrippers, bettered "Darce" in this department...

Highlight of the year for him was the one complete game he pitched on July 30th against the San Francisco Giants... it was his first ever in the majors and it stopped a record string of 45 straight non-complete games by the Reds staff...

He has a casual confidence in his pitching ability and never doubted for a moment that he'd end up in the majors...

Unlike most hurlers, the 25-year old Darcy focuses his attention on the number of innings he pitches rather than on his earned run average... "I figure any pitcher in the big leagues who pitches 250 or 300 innings, he's doing all right no matter what his record is. If you have a lot of innings in by the end of the season, you'll probably have a good earned run average," he says...

His idols in the game include Andy Messersmith of the Dogers and Gary Nolan... the latter's picture was tacked up in Pat's locker throughout the season... lives in Tucson, Arizona, during the off season... in Tuscon, he divides his time between attending school, doing volunteer work for a mental health clinic and working out for the next baseball season...

Pat is very meticulous about his personal appearance and is known for his very fine taste in clothing... was the first Red to have his hair texturized (curled)... his best friend in baseball is Greg Gross of the Houston Astros... during his free time, Pat reads light literature and plays chess... also enjoys listening to music...

danny driessen

Even though he enjoyed playing with a World Champion ballclub, Danny Driessen will probably not remember 1975 as his happiest season... he saw only part time duty at first base, right field and left field and came to bat only 210 times...

He has the most natural, unforced swing on the team, but has not had that much of a chance to use it... because of the uncoiling motion he has as he swings at the ball, he is called "The Cobra" by his teammates...

Although he can play several positions adequately, he is most at home at first base...

"Sleepy" (as he is also known) started off the year on the disabled list because of a hairline fracture of the left wrist he suffered while playing winter ball in Puerto Rico the previous January... he came off the injury quickly, proving that his swing was not damaged in any way...

Driessen is not known as a power hitter, but for the second consecutive year he socked seven home runs... and none of those were cheap shots...

Also, for the second consecutive year, he batted .281...

The 24-year old Driessen played third base in '74, and took a lot of flack from the press about his defensive slips... many feel that with a little more coaching and some added confidence, Danny could still be molded into a third sacker...

One of Danny's favorite stories is about how much athletic potential his brother William has... "There isn't any doubt in my mind if I can play I know he can play," he says. "I think he's a better all around player than I am. He plays first base, shortstop, the outfield -- he can play any position. He's a real good athlete"...

Danny's best friends on the club are Ed Armbrister and George Foster... like Foster, Driessen is a religious man... he is interested in health foods, but is not a fanatic on the subject... his dream for the future is owning a farm near his hometown of Hilton Head, South Carolina... his hobby is fishing...

rawly eastwick

Rawlins Jackson Eastwick, III -- the name could belong to a British golf pro or a New England yachtsman, but instead it belongs to the best young right-handed reliever in baseball... like fellow fireman, Will McEnaney, Rawly was trained almost exclusively as a reliever in his minor league days...

Eastwick was called up to the Reds from the Indianapolis farm club in late May of '75, and quickly established himself as one of the more consistent arms on the Cincinnati staff... his moving fastball and cool temperament made him the ideal man for Sparky Anderson to go to in the clutch...

"I'm a challenge pitcher," Eastwick says. "I relish the thought of going out and facing somebody with the bases loaded and nobody out. I don't get nervous or anything. In fact, I love to come into pressure situations"...

That enormous amount of self-reliance sees Rawly through the worst of situations on the mound...You've got to keep your confidence," he insists. "If you lose it, I don't care if you're a pitcher or catcher or third baseman, you're not going to be able to do anything."...Rawly's 22 saves and 41 game finishing efforts were staff highs...in'75, Eastwick mainly went with three pitches--fastball, slider andchange-up --and he experimented with a curve ball...

He was most happy with his slider, a pitch he uses with finesse... "I think it's a very good slider," the 25-year old native of Camden, New Jersy says. "Sometimes I do different speeds with it. I throw it like a curve ball sometimes. When I throw it hard, it's a very tough pitch to hit for righthanded and lefthanded hitters because it's got a short, sharp break on it. It's going to break in on a lefthander's fist and on a righthander, it's going to drop away from him"...

One of the reasons the Cincinnati organization is so fond of Rawly is his iron-man attitude toward his work... he would be the last man to go to the team trainer and complain of arm trouble... if he has any soreness, he's never told anybody about it...

During the season, Eastwick shared a home on Cincinnati's north side with several other guys, including Doug Flynn... one of his goals after the '75 campaign was to buy a home in the Queen City so he could live there all year around...

His biggest love off the diamond is painting... his simple compositions and natural themes are reminiscent of those painted by the celebrated master, Paul Cezanne...

doug flynn

The man most surprised to play in the big leagues in 1975 had to be Cincinnati reserve Doug Flynn... the smallish utility infielder had only been in the organization for three years and had made his name on his defensive talents when he showed up at the Reds '75 spring camp... but while in spring training, little Doug found himself at the plate... his hitting binge -- he led the club in hits in the exhibition season -- and his smooth infield play earned him a spot in the majors...

Sparky Anderson frequently compares Doug to Eddie Stanky, saying that both are players who can do many things for a club...

The twenty-four year old Flynn is very pleased to be with the Reds, as his hometown is Lexington, Kentucky and he has been following the play of the club for years...

Although most at home at shortstop, ''The Rook'' proved he could play second and third with equal grace... his .268 batting average in his first season with the Reds was quite a feat... he had never hit above .258 in the minor leagues...

He has exceptional bat control and was used often as a pinch-hitter in sacrifice situations... next to pitcher Don Gullett, Flynn may be the best bunter on the team...

Another unusual circumstance connected with Doug's arrival in the majors is the way that the veterans on the club took to him... Johnny Bench especially looked after the young fellow....

Baseball isn't the only sport that Flynn excells at... he is nearly a scratch golfer and was once considered a superior college basketball prospect...

Doug isn't the only Flynn who can be found in the Cincinnati clubhouse during the season... his father, Bob, is such a regular visitor that several Reds nailed a tag with his name on it above an empty locker... the elder Flynn won a golf tournament that the Reds players took part in... his son finished in second place... Bob is in the insurance business in Lexington, and while Doug isn't sure what kind of career he'll pursue when he gets out of baseball, he leans towards insurance or some kind of business...

He is one of the few single men on the club, and is said to be quite a charmer... Flynn is a very cheery young man, one who can hardly believe what is happening to him...

george foster

1975 must be marked down as the year that George Foster came of age in professional baseball... up until then, Foster had just been a benchwarmer with plenty of potential but little playing time... when Pete Rose moved into third base, Foster went to left field and so began the rumors that Sparky Anderson was a genius manager...

George so overwhelmed the fans in Riverfront that the left field section, once known as ''The Rose Garden,'' soon began calling itself ''Fosterville''...

In addition to adding nearly 40 points on to his '74 batting average, George also upped his home run production... his 23 homers were second on the club only to Johnny Bench's 28... and Bench went to bat 67 more times than Foster did... he delighted spectators with his casual, one-handed catches and his accurate pegs into the infield...

Much of George's success is due to the remarkable physical condition he keeps himself in... his concentration during the games is fierce...

Off the field, he is as sincere and moral a man as there is in the sports world... he has a deep sense of humanitarianism which is obvious in his behaviour... ''Yahtzee'' lives by a strong Christian credo... he spearheaded the organization of Sunday prayer meetings at Riverfront for the ballplayers... although he takes an active part in these Sunday meetings, he never sings along with the group... George admits that his voice ''sounds somewhat similar to gravel being crushed''...

He is an omnivorous reader, mostly of religious oriented material... one of his favorite topics of conversation is reincarnation... the fundamentals of hitting is another area George is well versed in...

During the season, George resides in a room at a local hotel, but he must move his belongings each time the club goes on a trip... the effect is that George is ''on the road'' from March until October...

His mother's home is in California, and she watches the Reds play in person in that area whenever she can...

George is a fastidious dresser, having rather conservative taste compared to most other ballplayers... seems to have a preference for knit pull-over shirts...

Has a very subtle sense of humor which his teammates appreciate...

His least favorite pastime is flying in airplanes, but he accepts it as part of being an athlete... he tries to sleep through as many flights as he can...

cesar geronimo

With a club that has four or five superstars and at least three others who are heading in that direction, it's sometimes easy to lose the Reds number eight hitter in the shadows... that's unfortunate, because Cesar Geronimo is unquestionably the league's strongest eighth batter...

Geronimo came to the Reds in the big deal with Houston in '71, and up until the '74 season, it looked like he was the only weak link the Reds acquired...

But '74 was the year Cesar matured into the ballplayer the Cincinnati brain trust suspected he would be... hitting low in the line-up a good deal of the time, "The Chief" came up with a .281 batting average with 54 RBI's... he followed up this offensive showing in '75 when he finished with .257 batting average, six home runs and 53 RBI's...

He has always possessed one of the most feared arms in the game... his pegs from deep centerfield to home are legendary among National Leaguers... in fact, Cesar's prized throwing arm almost kept him out of the outfield when he first got into professional ball... when the Yankees owned Geronimo back in the late '60's, they were so impressed with his arm that they gave a lot of thought to turning the native of the Dominican Republic into a pitcher... but Cesar's good work at the plate in spring training that year changed their minds... one reason that Cesar has been somewhat slow in his hitting development is the background he had in softball... in that game, he learned to upper-cut when swinging, and it's a habit he's had trouble shaking... but with the help of Reds batting instructor, Ted Kluszewski, Cesar has overcome it...

Like a few of his teammates, Cesar is a deeply religious man... before he began his baseball career, he spent some time in a seminary... generally he is a very quiet individual who keeps to himself... despite their occasional [and highly publicized] spats, his best friend on the team is Pedro Borbon... "The Chief" loves crossword puzzles, and can be located before most any game sitting in his locker working on one...

ken griffey

There may be some men with quicker reflexes and better base stealing savvy, but there is nobody in the National League who has more raw speed than the Reds rightfielder, Ken Griffey...

The muscular flash has been timed at 3.5 seconds going from home plate to first base on a drag bunt... this marvelous swiftness was the key to Ken's .305 batting average in '75... 38 of his 141 hits never left the infield...

'75 was his first full season in the majors, and his consistent hitting kept him in the number two slot in Sparky Anderson's line-up most of the time... in '73 and '74, ''Griff'' split his playing time between Cincinnati and their AAA affiliate, Indianapolis...

He was a little over anxious in the batters box in those years, tending to strike out too often... but in '75, he was put in the line-up and only occasionally was he platooned... although he fell short in '75, Griffey is committed to winning at least one batting title... is working with Joe Morgan to refine his base stealing tactics with the goal of getting 50 or more swipes a year...

He is a native of Donora, Pennsylvania, which is also the hometown of Stan Musial... quite naturally, he played the position of end on his high school football team... his future wife, Birdie, drove him in her car to his first baseball tryout... Birdie, who is also athletically inclined, helped shag balls at the tryout...

The Reds picked him in the 29th round in the June '69 summer free agent draft... even though Ken bats and throws lefthanded, he writes and eats with his right hand... his favorite food is chicken and creamed peas, which his wife claims he would eat three or four times a week if she would cook it that often...

During his free time, Ken works hard on pencil sketching... he has taken drawing lessons, and someday hopes to become a cartoonist...

One of his favorite pastimes before baseball games is swapping stories with his teammates... He has the most infectious laugh on the club... is something of a movie fan, especially Kung-Fu flicks...

don gullett

Sparky Anderson's favorite topic of conversation is this 24 year old lefthander... to Anderson, Don Gullett is the perfect example of what every young big league pitcher ought to be like, both on and off the field... Sparky is sure that this native son of Kentucky will wind up in the Hall of Fame, and after looking at Don's statistics, it would be hard to put up an argument... at his ripe tender age, he has already won 80 major league games... Warren Spahn hadn't even won his first game when he was 24...

"I have always been a winner and I always give everything I've got to contribute to a winning ballclub," Don says of himself... would probably have won 20 games in a season for the first time in his career in '75 had it not been for the broken left thumb he suffered on June 16... he missed two months and yet still managed to win 15 games...

He broke into the majors with the Reds in a big way against the Dodgers in 1970..."It was in Crosley Field and I think I pitched four plus innings to get my first win," Gullett says of his NL debut. "I also got a hit (a triple) in the game and stole a base. I think I was more nervous in that first game than at any other time"...

Going out to pitch for the Reds was something Don thought about doing while he was growing up in the hills of Eastern Kentucky... "I had always dreamed about a professional baseball career, and Cincinnati's always been my favorite team, being so close to home -- and my father was a big fan of Cincinnati. Just listening to those guys and wondering what it would be like... it was just like a dream come true"...

He is an extremely competitive fellow, whether he's on the mound or at the plate... most certainly is the best fielding and hitting pitcher in the NL... his best pitch is still his blazing fastball, but he is learning to compliment it with some off-speed stuff... his forkball may be the best slow pitch he has...

Because he never has too much to say, his teammates call him "Gabby"... his other nickname -- "Smokin' Don"-- came about because of the speed of his pitches... Gullett is a devoted sportsman in the off season, as he can't seem to get enough fishing and hunting...

clay kirby

When the Reds gathered in Tampa, Florida in March of '75 for spring training, one young righthander was the most optimistic man on the Cincinnati pitching staff... Clay Kirby, who had been traded to the Reds from the San Diego Padres in late '73, was convinced that he was going to make his mark in the big leagues that year... "I thought I pitched well for the Reds in '74," Clay said. "I didn't get many runs scored for me and circumstances in different games caused me not to win. But I'm going to win 20 games this year. Before I would say that I 'hoped' I was going to win 20 -- I'm not going to go with the feeling of 'hoping' to do it, I'm just going to go do it"...

But somewhere along the line, Clay's plans went awry... a little arm trouble and some bad breaks kept the hard throwing Kirby on the bench a good deal of the time... he was used mainly as a spot starter and long reliever... he still won 10 of his 16 decisions... "The Kid" had a six game winning streak in July and August...

His troubles on the mound seemed to stem from a few too many gopher balls and wild pitches... and when he got into trouble, he got the "quick hook" from Sparky Anderson... Kirby took it all in stride, his confidence in his pitching ability apparently unshaken...

Clay got an early start in sports, as he began to really take baseball seriously when he was about six years old... "there was nothing else to do where I lived," Kirby says...

The story of how Clay first became interested in pitching has a Dizzy Dean flavor to it... "I used to live on a dead end street next to a little creek," Kirby recalls. "Across the creek was a railroad track. When trains used to come by, we would throw rocks at the train. I could always hit the train more than anybody else could"... Clay had such a powerful arm when he was a child that he could heave the ball from centerfield over the back-stop behind home plate...

Hunting and fishing are two of Kirby's chief non-baseball interests...

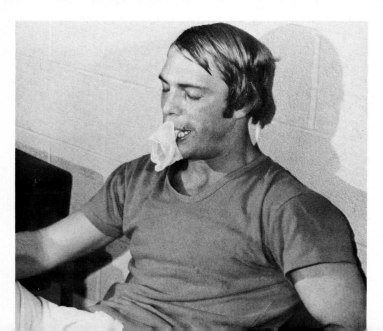

will mcenaney

The most important quality that a relief pitcher has to possess is the ability to deliver a strike whenever he needs to... and Will McEnaney, the Reds number one lefthanded fireman, can do just that... Will's control in '75 was excellent, as he gave up just 23 free passes in 91 innings pitched...

"I've got four or five All Star ballplayers out there and I know that if it's hit at them that 99 chances out of 100 they're going to make that good play for me," Will explains. "So when you've got that on your mind, you're not afraid to get a hitter to hit the ball. When you've got seven guys behind you and an All Star catcher in front of you, you can't help but feel relaxed"...

The 23-year old native of Springfield, Ohio, was relaxed enough in the Reds championship season to net 5 wins in 7 decisions, have a 2.47 ERA and be credited with 15 saves... Will was used mostly in short relief stints...

Although the lithe McEnaney is content with his role of bullpen ace, deep in his heart he someday would like to get a shot at starting... "Relief pitching has gotten me here and I can't complain," he says. "I'm happy with my job and I'm still going to get paid the same whether I'm a starter or a reliever, so I can't say anything against it. But I would like to give starting a try, just to see how it would go. Just out of curiosity, I'd like to give it a try sometime"...

McEnaney is kind of a flaky fellow, one who is not afraid to pull a harmless practical joke... he is the proud owner of a custom van -- a kind of cross between a mobile home and a camper... on the advice of several people, including Willie Stargell of the Pittsburgh Pirates, McEnaney had the van redone to the point where it can do everything but fly...

Will is articulate, so during the winter of '75, he spent much time giving talks to groups... his teammates call him "Face" because he reminds them of the great hurler, Elroy Face...

joe morgan

The dynamo of the Big Red Machine, Joe Morgan, had a dream campaign in 1975... for the first time in his career, he hit over .300... his .327 batting average was tops on the Cincinnati club... the thirty-two year old Morgan drove in 94 RBI's, also a career high mark... probably would have driven home over 100 runners if he had batted third in the line-up all season... once again he was a demon on the basepaths, as he swiped 60 bags...

He's not the fastest man on the team, but he has that rare instinct for reading pitchers and taking off at the right time... oddly enough, he gets his biggest leads off lefthanders... against a southpaw, Joe figures he gets a lead off first base of about 15 feet, whereas against a righthander his lead is about 14 feet... "Everything's right out in front of you," he says. "A righthander has his back to you, but with a lefty, you can see everything."...

He is very firm about getting his lead, emphasizing that he won't be intimidated by the pitcher... "I control my lead, not the pitcher," Morgan asserts. "The pitcher's got to go to the plate sometime"...

Little Joe drew 132 walks in '75, a club record... his defensive work at second earned him his third Golden Glove... as was expected, Morgan won the National League's Most Valuable Player Award for '75... he is the most complete ballplayer in the game today, and could probably play for any team in any era...

His most peculiar habit on the diamond is the way he flaps his elbows as he stands waiting for the pitch in the batters box... it was a habit that grew out of Nellie Fox's advice of how to remember to keep his elbow out when swinging...

He says that he is a "moody" player, but Morgan is generally very talkative... may be the easiest and most cooperative interview subject in the NL... always takes time to explain his philosophy of the game to anyone who is interested...

He is an intelligent man who attends college part-time in the off season... like his good friend, Willie Stargell, Joe is a wine connoisseur... also has fine taste in music... his nickname is "Sweet Pea"... is a flashy dresser, and at one time thought about opening a clothing shop near his winter home in Oakland, California... has an enchanting wife, Gloria, and two cute daughters....

gary nolan

When the Cincinnati Reds finally won that elusive World Championship in October of 1975, there couldn't have been a happier player on the club than Gary Nolan... the twenty-seven year old righthander wasn't happy just because he was part of the best squad in the majors-- he was happy just to be in baseball at all...

Nolan was one of the game's phenom's when he won 14 of 22 decisions and fanned 206 batters in 1967... from that year through the first half of 1972, Gary was one of the aces of the ailing Cincinnati staff... but just before the All Star game in '72, he experienced some pain in his right shoulder and the success story took a bend... the next two years were nightmares: he pitched in two games for Cincinnati in '73 and then the bottom fell completely out in '74... the fortunes changed later in '74 for Nolan when he underwent surgery to have a calcium spur removed from the sore shoulder... he reported back to Indianapolis near the end of the '74 season and hurled 6 innings in 2 games... in those two games, Gary found that the pain had disappeared... after the season was over, he went to the Instructional League and pitched 45 innings... the work helped build up his shoulder enough so that he was ready to try the big leagues again...

It was like a miracle in spring training '75... that marvelous control of Nolan's was still there after all that time off... he zipped through the '75 season, winning 15 and losing 9 with an ERA of 3.16... Gary walked only 29 batters, and unbelievable as it may seem, he led the club in innings pitched with 211... Sparky Anderson has predicted that Nolan will even be better in 1976...

Gary is known as a "thinking man's pitcher" who seldom beats himself... in the dugout, he's one of the real spirit men on the team...

One of his best friends on the Reds is Don Gullett, the man he rooms with when the club travels... he and Gullett spend much time going over other club's hitters, probing that helps them both out...

He is called "Sarge" by his fellow Reds... is a very concerned citizen who has worked with young people in the off season...

fred norman

If the pitchers in the National League were rated according to their guile, little Fred Norman would receive the number one ranking... his assortment of pitches and the clever way he uses them is enough to keep any hitter off stride...

Most Red followers think of the dancing screwball as Freddie's best pitch, but the 33-year old lefthander claims that it isn't... "Overall I would say my curve is my best pitch," Fred says. "It's got a very quick break"... he likes the reputation of relying primarily on the screwball... "It's good to have batters looking for my screwball, then I can get away with my fastball," he comments... Norman estimates that he throws the screwball about twenty per cent of the time, his curve ball another twenty per cent and his fastball the other sixty per cent... once in awhile, he mixes in a sharp slider...

He is known for his streaks of dazzling pitching... when he came to the Reds from the San Diego Padres in '73, Cincinnati was struggling in fourth spot in their division... Fred immediately came up with the big effort... he threw two consecutive shutouts and just missed tossing a third one... he won nine of his first eleven decisions... he put a similar streak together the last three months of the '75 season... during July, August and September he won nine out of ten and had an ERA of below 3.00... those were important victories for the Reds, as pitching ace Don Gullett was injured during part of that time and the club needed all the mound support that could be mustered...

But life in baseball hasn't all been easy sailing for the man the Reds call "Smooth"... bouncing around between the major and the minors, dealing with a congenital back problem and sore arm troubles have tested Norman's determination several times... but his fierce pride and desire to contribute something to baseball have kept him going...

The turning point in his career came in 1971 when he played for Tulsa... it was there that Warren Spahn taught him the screwball, the one pitch that solidified him as a major league hurler...

In the off season, Freddie travels and plays a lot of golf... he is a very eligible bachelor...

tony perez

The Cincinnati Reds are an exceptionally close group who mesh as well as any team in the game... one of the central figures in this unit, one of those who really brings the men together is Tony Perez... he's the kind of fellow it is impossible not to like... Perez continually kids his fellow Reds about their performance on the field and this kind of joking goes a long way in keeping the mood in the clubhouse loose... of course, Tony is one of the most talented athletes on the team...

The 33-year old first baseman was almost dealt away before the '75 season, but that trade is the one Reds President Bob Howsam will forever be thankful he didn't make... "The Big Dog" was again the big terror among NL hurlers... he drove in 109 runners, the third time in a row that he's topped the century mark and the ninth consecutive time he's gone over 90... in fact, he's the only active player with 90 or more RBI's in the last nine seasons... it was during '75 that Perez became the all time Cincinnati run producer... he passed Frank Robinson on the list when he clicked with his 1010th run driven in... he continued to be the best clutch hitter on the club... tense moments seem to bring the best out in him...

His steadying influence is most obvious in Dave Concepcion, Tony's roommate on the road... Perez can always bounce back after a bad day, and he's been able to teach Davey to do the same... Tony's only noticeable reaction to a Cincinnati losing streak is that he stays up a little later at night, reading cowboy magazines to take his mind off things...

He has a robust sense of humor and is seldom seen without a grin on his face... he really likes western movies...

There is only one way to describe his wife Pituka -- pure class... she's a very well groomed lady who is as cheerful as her husband... she also happens to be an excellent cook, which works out well for Tony because he is a most appreciative eater... Paella, a sea food dish, is Pituka's specialty... one of the few foods which Tony doesn't care for is cheese...

He is a very devoted family man... the Perez clan lives in an apartment near the beach in Santurce, Puerto Rico... they spend much of the winter swimming and enjoying the warm climate... they also enjoy traveling in the off season...

bill plummer

Bill Plummer's biggest fan in baseball is the man he plays behind -- Johnny Bench... there isn't anybody around who appreciates the frustration and anguish of playing in back of the number one catcher in the game better than that number one catcher... but "Plumb" is a patient man who is satisfied with his back-up role and he does whatever he can for the club when he gets his chances...

Bill was in 65 games in '75, coming to the plate a total of 159 times... the 7 doubles he hit in the year tied his major league high mark in that category... and the 19 RBI's he collected in '75 was his best big league total... two of his 29 hits were game winners...

Bill came to the Reds from the Chicago Cubs along with Clarence Jones and Ken Myette for Ted Abernathy in January of 1969... he played in Indianapolis for most of his next four seasons, hitting a career high of .266 with the Indians in 1971... the next season he joined the Reds full time to become Johnny Bench's understudy...

One of his most unusual experiences in baseball took place when he was with Indianapolis in '69... he went to the mound and pitched for 2 innings, giving up 2 hits a walk and no runs...

Bill is a giant of a man at 6-1 and 200 pounds... he looks like a well-shaped weight lifter... he's as gentle a person as there is in sports... Plumb is very quiet, going about his business and disturbing no one... there is no harder a worker on the club, as Bill frequently comes in early and does some extra training... many of the pitchers on the team insist that next to Bench, Plummer is the finest receiver they've ever pitched to...

Bill is the son of William L. Plummer, a man who pitched in the minors for six years in the 20's... he is also the nephew of "Red" Baldwin, a former minor league catcher...

Aside from hunting during the off seasons, he also works on his father-in-law's ranch in California...

The twenty-eight year old Plummer has about three years of college work in, and hopes to finish up a degree when he gets out of baseball...

merv rettenmund

One of the reasons that the Big Red Machine rolled to a World Championship in 1975 was the fine bench strength of the team... Sparky Anderson, a manager who likes to mix all sorts of line-up combinations, had the men to do it in '75... one of those who contributed a lot in a reserve role was Merv Rettenmund...

Merv was traded to the Reds with Junior Kennedy and Bill Wood from Baltimore for Ross Grimsley and Wallace Williams in the winter of 1973... in his first season with the team, Rettenmund just couldn't get adjusted... he frankly admits that it "was really a bad year"... he hit just .216 in 80 games... but Merv came roaring back in '75... he filled in for Ken Griffey in right field on occasion and hit very well...

Merv's experience against the Boston Red Sox and his previous Series play served as good source material for other Red players during the fall classic...

The thirty-two year old Rettenmund has had a brilliant baseball career... his best seasons came in 1970 and 1971 when he was with Baltimore... he hit over .300 both of those years and was a key man in Oriole attack... he has now played in five Championship Series and four World Series...

He rates the '75 confrontation between the Red Sox and the Reds as one of the best... "Every World Series is a little different, but this was far and away the most exciting," he says of the '75 encounter...

Merv and his wife Sue own a home in the Queen City and plan to live there for a few years even if Merv moves along to another team... "It's centrally located," he says. "My wife has in-laws and my in-laws are not too far away. And it's good to have roots no matter what your business is"...

Sue Rettenmund is co-owner of a needlepoint store in Cincinnati which is quite appropriately named the Threadneedle Street... she and Merv are genuine gourmets and Merv can name an exciting restaurant in every big league town...

He is the number one tennis buff on the Cincinnati team... other activities that Merv enjoys are reading [mostly best sellers] and playing cards...

His nickname is "Marvelous Merv"... when he retires, Merv would like to try coaching a college baseball team...

pete rose

At thirty-four years of age, Pete Rose plays the game of baseball as if he were a plucky teenager... he never stops hustling, no matter if he's chasing a fly ball or running down to first after drawing a walk... his value to the Reds is inestimable... he never lets up when it comes to baseball, and he simply will not tolerate any of his fellow players letting up either... the title of captain of the team is something Pete doesn't take lightly... when a young player makes the Reds, he knows he's going to have to work his tail off to even stay close to Rose-- and that's the kind of example by a star athlete that General Managers dream about....

In '75, Pete bounced back from his first sub-.300 season to hit .317... Rose had broken a string of nine consecutive .300 or better seasons in '74 when he hit "just" .284... he had 210 hits in '75, the seventh time in his career that he's gone over the 200 notch... he led the National League in doubles with 47... it was the second straight year he's been at the top of the loop in doubles... he scored 112 runs, the fourth year in a row and the sixth overall that he's passed the 100 mark...

But all of these hitting achievements don't begin to reflect what Pete Rose brings to a ballclub... his daring move from the outfield to third base on May 3 gave the Reds a new third baseman and installed George Foster in left field... if any one thing turned Cincinnati around, that move did it... Rose worked on his fielding endlessly, and developed into a more than adequate third sacker... by the end of the year, he was among the top two or three hot corner men in the league... after spring training in '76, Rose promises he'll be even better at defense... when Pete is presented a challenge like the move to third, he becomes a tiger... he played in 162 games despite a minor arm pain which was the result of the different kind of throw he had to make from third...

Pete's very colorful wife, Karolyn, is as delightfully unique as Rose himself... they have two winsome children, son Pete and daughter Fawn... Karolyn is looked upon as the unofficial "captain" of the players wives...

Pete is as aggressive in business as he is in baseball... he owns a very successful family restaurant in the Western Hills area of Cincinnati... he eats there frequently which contributes to the popularity of the place...

He likes to participate in all sports... is particularly skilled at table tennis... he doesn't make a big deal of it, but Pete does as much for needy causes as anyone on the club... he's especially good to young journalists...

Was named Sportsman of the Year by Sports Illustrated... manager Sparky Anderson says that "Charlie Hustle" will be a first ballot Hall of Famer...

WE WON, WE WON! -- A teary-eyed, exultant Will McEnaney has just induced Carl Yastrzemski to fly out to Cesar Geronimo for the final out of the 1975 World Series. Johnny Bench and Pete Rose join in the ecstasy of Cincinnati's first title in 35 years.

1975 cincinnati reds

Back Row, left to right: Dan Driessen, Darrel Chaney, Ken Griffey, Gary Nolan, Dave Concepcion, Ed Armbrister, Clay Carroll, Will McEnaney, Terry Crowley, Cesar Geronimo, Don Gullett.

Middle Row: Bernie Stowe, Equipment Manager; Paul Campbell, Traveling Secretary; Johnny Bench, Bill Plummer, Clay Kirby, George Foster, Jack Billingham, Tom Carroll, Pat Darcy, Rawly Eastwick, Tony Perez, Pedro Borbon, Larry Starr, Trainer.

Front Row: Pete Rose, Joe Morgan, Ted Kluszewski, Coach; Alex Grammas, Coach; Sparky Anderson, Manager; George Scherger, Coach; Larry Shepard, Coach; Fred Norman, Doug Flynn, Merv Rettenmund. Seated in front Tim McGinn, Bat Boy.

hal mccoy

Hal McCoy, 35, has covered the Cincinnati Reds, home and away, regularly for three seasons as Baseball Writer for The Dayton Daily News.

McCoy, a 1962 graduate of Kent State University's School of Journalism, has won 14 national and state writing awards.

In addition to covering the Reds during baseball season, he writes a regular column for the Daily News.

In his 13 years of sports journalism, McCoy has covered The Masters, PGA and U. S. Open golf tournaments, the Indianapolis 500 and Daytona 500, the Rose Bowl, the NCAA and NIT basketball tournaments, the Cleveland Browns on a regular basis and assorted other varied sporting events.

Hal, his wife Linda, and their two sons, Brian [12] and Brent [4], reside in West Carrollton, Ohio, where McCoy makes almost daily appearances on the tennis court.

earl lawson

Earl Lawson began his newspaper career as a copyboy with the old Cincinnati Times-Star as a 17-year-old fresh out of high school. Within two years he was a full-fledged reporter on the paper's city-side news staff.

The following three years were spent in the U. S. Army where, Lawson, as a member of the 96th Infantry Division, made assault landings on Leyte and Okinawa in the South Pacific.

After his discharge as a first sergeant, Lawson returned to the Times-Star, joining the paper's sports department. Three years later, 1949, Lawson made his first trip with the Cincinnati Reds. The following year he succeeded the late Frank Y. Grayson as the Times-Star's baseball writer.

In 1958 the Times-Star was bought by the Cincinnati Post, and Lawson continued as the Post's baseball writer.

During the past 25 years, Lawson, in addition to covering the Reds for his paper, has been a regular correspondent for The Sporting News, and has written numerous pieces for magazines, including the old Saturday Evening Post, Sport, and True.

dennis gruelle

Dennis Gruelle, who provided the bulk of the photography for this book, was born in 1952 in Livermore, California. He graduated from Illinois State University with a Bachelor's Degree in Psychology in 1973. Along with William Matthews and Peter Alexis, he founded THE REDS ALERT newspaper in 1974. He remains as Editor and chief photographer for the baseball newspaper. Mr. Gruelle currently lives in Cincinnati.

bill matthews

William E. Matthews, publisher of The Relentless Reds, is a native of Shelbyville, Ky., and a 1952 graduate of the University of Michigan. Following nine years' service with the Central Intelligence Agency, he entered the newspaper business in 1962 with the acquisition of The Shelby Sentinel, Shelbyville.

After serving as president of Newspapers, Inc., from 1968 to 1973, and its successor, Landmark Community Newspapers, Inc., from 1973 to 1975, he organized PressCo, Inc.

PressCo, Inc. publishes THE REDS ALERT, a weekly sports magazine focusing on the Cincinnati Reds, Bengals, and Stingers; The Grant County News, a weekly newspaper located in Williamstown, Ky.; and a group of publications promoting the state park systems and tourism in Kentucky and Tennessee.

Matthews and his wife, Else, have four children -- Beau, Ellen Baxter, Bland Ballard, and a married daughter, Lisa Matthews Griffith.

pete alexis

Peter Alexis, who wrote the team profiles for this volume, was born in Danville, Illinois in 1949. He graduated from Illinois State University with a Master's Degree in Clinical Psychology in 1973. In March of 1974, he co-founded the weekly baseball newspaper, THE REDS ALERT. Mr. Alexis lives in Cincinnati and continues to serve as Editor of the baseball publication.